The Wealthy Preacher

Proverbs 10:22

Laurence Croswell

The
Wealthy
Preacher

Laurence Croswell

PUBLISHING

Belleville, Ontario, Canada

The Wealthy Preacher

Copyright © 1996, Laurence Croswell

All Scripture quotations, unless otherwise specified, are taken from *The King James Version* of the Bible.

Scriptures marked NIV are from the *New International Version* of the Bible (Copyright © 1973, 1978, 1984 International Bible Society. Used by permission of Zondervan Bible Publishers. All rights reserved.)

ISBN: 1-896400-22-1

Essence Publishing is a Christian Book Publisher dedicated to furthering the work of Christ through the written word. For more information, contact: 103B Cannifton Rd., Belleville, ON, Canada K8N 4V2.
Phone: 1-800-238-6376 • Fax: (613) 962-3055
Email: essence@intranet.on.ca
Internet: http://www.essence.on.ca

Printed in Canada
by

Essence
PUBLISHING

Table of Contents

Acknowledgements

his book is a collection of devotional readings that were written over several years as illustrations of spiritual truths. Many of the stories were used on Sunday mornings as I preached to the congregation of Centennial Road Standard Church. Some of these stories are about members of our congregation; others are about my wife, Faye, and sons, Mark and Darren. I am grateful to all who allowed me to put their lives on display to make Bible truths come alive.

Many people made this book possible for publication:

Linda Tennant keyed in the type and made corrections, over and over again, as we read and re-read the manuscript. Her patience and kind spirit are appreciated more than she will ever know.

A special thank you to Keith Heine who did the cover design, and Mark Lysko who was the photographer. You can't judge a book by its cover, but if you could, this book would be a number one seller!

Dawn Dewick, a former colleague at Prince of Wales School, read the first draft and made corrections. Of all things, she passed it on to our friend, Sheila Tamblyn, who taught across the hall. What would you expect? Sheila agreed with Dawn, and I had to succumb to all the suggestions.

Faye read the manuscript for the final time. Her suggestions were bold and daring, but she could do it – she's my wife! I appreciate all her work in helping me with the writing style.

A special word of appreciation to all the good people at Centennial Road Standard Church. They listen to me preach Sunday after Sunday. They are saints! They are the inspiration for many of these stories.

1

The Wealthy Preacher

he *Financial Post* has an 86-year tradition of being the business voice of people-in-the-know. So, when a complimentary copy landed in my mailbox, I gasped in astonishment. Bold headlines loudly proclaimed:

LAURENCE CROSWELL TRIUMPHS ONCE AGAIN!

I quickly tore off the plastic wrap to read the important story inside: "Smart Lyn resident will get free FP attaché, FOUR WEEKS FREE, plus 18% SAVINGS, by starting delivery now on Canada's BUSINESS VOICE."

It was a promotional gag. A subscription drive. I had not impressed Bay Street or Wall Street with my investment prowess. I had not been privy to the week's biggest business stories. I was only one of numerous names purchased as subscription prospects. Nevertheless, I must confess to a tinge of exhilaration at seeing my name in such prestigious headlines. *Financial Post* knows it. Smart campaign offer!

But I know better. I'm not a mover and a shaker on the investment scene. I don't have an inside track to experts in the financial markets. But I am wealthy! Not the way *Financial Post* counts wealth – in terms of investments, bank accounts, and cold cash.

Every day, I have the privilege of reading a book of instructions written by the One who created me and loves me. He gives me thoughts and advice on how to be successful and filled with joy. And He is only a prayer away. Unbelievable!

Each evening, I sit across the table from a lovely lady who prepares a delicious meal and invites me to join her for a romantic dinner and stimulating conversation. She puts up with all my idiosyncrasies, and still says she loves me. Incredible!

Two boys call me Dad. One plays the piano and, periodically, I hear the strains of Johann Sebastian Bach, or George Frederic Handel – on off days, played without mistakes. Completely enjoyable! The other plays football, and even scored a touchdown. I was ecstatic!

Every Sunday, I attend a wonderful church filled with some of the greatest people in the world. They sing and clap their hands and listen to me teach from the Bible. It's almost like heaven!

I work with the best church staff ever assembled (and I mean it!). They are always stretching me with their faith, and they trust me enough to call me "Pastor." I'm not sure why. I don't deserve all these blessings. I think I'm GOD'S SPOILED KID! Not that I'm questioning or complaining. Just praising!

So *Financial Post* may be closer than they think. My life is triumphant. Blessed. When I count my many blessings – name them one by one – I know that I'm a wealthy man.

Imagine, a wealthy preacher! Incredible!

🎜 GROWING RICH

Psalm 37; Psalm 107:1-9

🎜 INVESTING WISELY

Search an old hymnal for the song, "Count Your Blessings." Read the words. Sing them. Give thanks with a grateful heart.

2

Child of the Garden

arold Moyles. Leathery face. Calloused hands. Piercing blue eyes. His long, bony fingers had seeded acres and acres of sweet corn... plucked dozens and dozens of the plump cobs to sell on the farmers' market or the back streets of Brockville. He was a child of the garden.

He was also an institution. The famous "Corn Man." Police looked the other way when Harold's tractor and wagon wheeled into a NO PARKING zone. Loyal customers crowded around to buy a delicious dozen from the darkly-tanned old farmer in his bib-overalls, his straw hair tossing in the wind.

But not any more. His new frontier is a locked ward. The dewy mornings in the corn patch are misty memories. The crisp, fresh air is all but forgotten. The antiseptic breath of the special care unit reminds me that the child of the garden is now captive to old age and dementia.

Mine was the unhappy task of leaving him at the lodge. Before turning to go, I watched the old man, his few wisps of white hair combed neatly across his bony head. He sat hunched at his table... huddled like an old gunny sack thrown over a pile of bleached buffalo bones.

I turned to go, and gave a feeble wave to the forlorn old man at the table. I tried to swallow the gravelly lump wedged tightly in my throat. Despite his tangled memory, it seemed so unfair to leave him there. Harold had given so much and owned so little – every profit he had made had been returned to the Bible College where he had lived since 1931.

But now the garden is gone. The field of curly tassels no longer waves to the smiling sun. Harold's robust hymn in the crisp dawn of the corn patch is silent. Only memories live on.

"Lord," I sighed, "what lesson would you have me learn from my visit to the lodge? Why is it so hard to leave the old man at the table? Why the loneliness inside my heart? The tears? And why the empty garden?"

Insight came in an unexpected way. Still wrapped in melancholic contemplation, I heard a sob. Startled, I paused to hear the voice. Someone else was sorrowing over another empty garden.

"Surely you will understand my loneliness," said the Voice. "You left an old man in a lodge because he needed care, but I left the children of My creation because they decided to reject My care. And the garden is empty. The evening chats by the gurgling brook are past. No more songs of praise beneath the Tree of Life."

God must have wept when He turned His back to walk away.

🐾 GROWING RICH

Genesis 3; Romans 5:1-11

🐾 INVESTING WISELY

Set aside time today for private contemplation. Perhaps sit in your favourite chair, walk in the quiet woods or park, or kneel at your bedside. Meditate on God's love in that while you were a sinner – a rebel who walked out on God – Christ died for you. Give thanks.

3

Not Glamorous, But Glorious

Bette doesn't hold any office in our church. She doesn't sit on any board, or even sing in the choir. Her manner is modest and demure, and she walks with a pained limp. Few people would even know her name if they bumped into her. But Bette is saint material. Pure gold and all heart.

Last night, Bette shared a letter with us. She couldn't keep it to herself. I read it and wept – for joy and gratitude, not sorrow and pain. Let me give you some background:

Bette is a widow. Her husband, Bill, was not outwardly religious. But he had faith, the quiet kind. And he had heart.

Bill was in the armed forces, stationed in northern Canada, an isolated and desolate region. He had a habit of inviting lonely airforce kids home for some of Bette's home cooking – a break from the barren drudgery of barracks and the radar-tracking classes that he taught. One student was an eighteen-year-old girl whose name was also Betty. Bill noted that this pretty girl was troubled, her face clouded. No laughter and sparkle. "Why not come for supper tonight?" he urged.

It only was a short while until Bette held the weeping teenager in her arms and heard the awful truth. She was pregnant. Armed force's policy in those days: immediate discharge.

Most couples would have clucked their tongues and said, "Too bad this happened to such a nice girl" – and then forgotten about her. But not Bill and Bette. The young girl was desolate. Her parents told her not to come home. So, Bill and Bette said, "Stay with us." Abortion was not an option. Six weeks later, Bill was sleeping on the couch, and the young mother-to-be was sharing Bette's bed. The Charlton's two young children occupied the only other bedroom allotted to service families.

Two months quickly passed, and suddenly one January morn, Bill was driving through a snowy storm with a mother-in-labour by his side. Soon a new member joined the crowded Charlton household: Baby James (Jim) William.

For two months, Bette scrounged baby clothes and furniture, and hunted for an apartment. A kind Salvation Army officer came to the rescue, and soon the baby and mom were living in their own small home.

It wasn't easy. The young mother babysat for money. Upgraded through correspondence. For four years, her son received hand-me-downs from Randy – Bill and Bette's little son. And then she moved West. Home. Got a better job. Put her son through school. Jim became a teacher.

Years later, Bette opened this letter and read:

My Dearest Bette,

My thoughts of you and Bill have been so deep today. This evening at 6:05 p.m., Mary and Jim were blessed with an 8 lb. 10 oz. baby boy. I am a grandmother! I owe this miracle to you and Bill.

It is 11 p.m. and I have spent the last 5 hours reliving my past. I shudder to think what my life could have been like if I hadn't turned to you for comfort and advice.

My heart is always so full of love for you and Bill. I remember when I got brave enough to confide in you, and you put your arms around me and told me we would find a solution. At that moment, I could not have loved you more.

You know how I feel about Bill. What a kind, loving man! I have never met another like him. The baby is named after him, just as Jim was: Ryan William.

Remember when Jim graduated from university and I said how I wished Bill were here so we could tell him? You wrote back and said, "Bill knows." Well, through your faith in God and me, I know Bill knows about the baby.

I will send an announcement and picture when we get them. I had to drop you a line immediately.

You did so many kind things for so many people and I know you will never change. What a comforting thing to know!

We all love you. God bless you. I am so happy!

Gratefully yours,

Love, Betty

Reminds me a lot of Tabitha (Dorcas) in Acts 9. Her name meant "gazelle" – a beautiful graceful deer. But what was beautiful about Tabitha was her works of love among needy people. Seemed like a tragedy when she fell sick and died. Impoverished women stood about her body, weeping and showing the garments she had made. There was no social assistance for widows and single mothers in that culture. Then Peter arrived on the scene. "Tabitha, arise," he said. He took her by the hand, and presented her alive.

I wish more Tabithas and Bettes would arise. A lot more Jims and Ryans would stand and call them blessed. They would also qualify for a Prophet's Reward – just like Jesus said.

Not glamorous work, but a glorious reward!

GROWING RICH

Matthew 10:37-42; Acts 9:36-42

INVESTING WISELY

Organize a ministry work force to help single mothers and widows. Offer practical helps like babysitting, car mechanics and house repairs.

4
Finding My Roots

ebecca Hobbs may have been the old woman who lived in the shoe with so many children she didn't know what to do. Rebecca cared for twenty-four in her life time!

Rebecca lived in the crowded city of Leeds, England, in one of the earliest cities to be transformed by the Industrial Revolution. She married a brickmaker by the name of Charles Croswell, and the two newly-weds settled down to eke out a living among the roaring factories and damp tenements of the smog-filled city. There was the constant fear of unemployment and near starvation. So, in 1842, the Croswells decided to pack up their children, now numbering eight, and join thousands of their countrymen emigrating to North America with the dream of a better life and fresh air.

But the voyage was long and treacherous. Menacing icebergs drifting into the cold Labrador current delayed progress. An epidemic of ship's fever (cholera) broke out on board the little sailing vessel and many of the passengers and crew died during the thirteen weeks it took to cross the Atlantic. Rebecca's little baby died, and just three days out of Montreal, so did her husband. But despite her grief, Rebecca offered to nurse the infant of George French, whose own wife had also succumbed to the dreaded cholera.

Disembarking at Montreal, the two families proceeded together by barge and steamboat to the bustling town of Dundas, Upper Canada. The eventual marriage of Rebecca and George was not, it seems, simply a marriage of convenience, but one of sympathy and affection. But wedding bells meant a joint family of fifteen hungry mouths. Eight more were born – a grand total of twenty-four children, counting the infant who died on board the ship.

George and Rebecca took risks by leaving England, and they faced the adversities and consequences of that decision. They each lost a mate they loved, but found love again in each other. They worked hard to give their children a good life in a new land, and flourished as circumstances permitted. Their descendants owe them a great deal. I know. Rebecca was my great, great grandmother.

SPIRITUAL ROOTS

Many years previous, in the grey dawn of history, another couple grew restless in the city of their surroundings. His name was Abraham and her name was Sarah. They grew up amid the smog and smut of an idolatrous, evil people. Abraham's sensitive spirit protested against the evil practices, not only of his home city of Ur, but also of his father's own house.

At last God appeared unto him. "Leave your country and your kindred. Come to a land which I will show you."

It was no small matter for Abraham to pull up roots, tear himself away from his nearest and dearest, and start for a land which, as yet, he did not know. But the key to Abraham's success was obedience. And God promised that He would make of Abraham a great nation and a blessing to all the families of the earth.

Dangers and hardships lurked along the way. Faith was severely tested. There were tears. Heartache. Frustration. Ultimately, we focus in on a tottery old man nearing a century mark, but still clutching the dream that he would father a nation. His son was still to be born.

Abraham was faithful to his vision. Confused at times and baffled at others, he held to God's promise of a land and a people. But when hope seemed impossible, Sarah bore Abraham a son in his old age, and the laughter that filled the patriarch's tent made the aged pair forget their long and weary wait. Abraham called his son Isaac; his name meant "laughter."

ROOTS ARE IMPORTANT

Rebecca and Charles give me historical roots, but Abraham and Sarah give me spiritual roots. Abraham is the spiritual father of those who believe (Rom. 4:11). Sarah herself received strength to conceive seed, and she bore a child when she was past age because she judged God faithful (Heb. 11:11).

Quite a pedigree, I'd say!

♟ GROWING RICH

Genesis 12, 13, 15-18, 21:1-8

♟ INVESTING WISELY

Some thoughts for meditation:

1. *Tough people face hard times with tough determination.*

2. *People of faith don't look back.*

3. *Unselfish people don't give in to self-pity.*

QUESTION: *How do these thoughts apply to my life?*

5
Gone Fishing

mart-aleck fish! Somehow they have ESP when my hook is in the water, and they ignore it.

Why, just this morning, my friend, Gord, and I went fishing for lake trout. He carefully snapped two identical "Johnny Green" lures to the lines on our rods. Fresh sunfish tails camouflaged the vicious hooks dangling on the end. Gord handed one rod to me, and we began to troll and jig across the lake.

"Got one!" Gord grunted as his rod began to quiver.

I watched with secret envy as he reeled in the shining beauty. Six times he repeated the ritual. Even threw three back because he judged them too small.

Me? Four hours of jigging my line back and forth across Charleston Lake, and all I had to display was one partially decomposed clam shell and a piece of soggy bark.

When we finally pulled the boat back into Gord's yard, I thanked him for taking me along to his favourite fishing spot and turned to go, empty-handed. But Gord stopped me. "Here," he said, "Take these home for a fish dinner." He thrust the three already filleted trout into my hand. I hesitated, but Gord insisted.

Tonight, I faced my family with dignity. My two sons' jibes about Dad's competency with a fishing rod were muffled by the sizzling aroma of frying fish in an iron skillet.

HARD DAY'S NIGHT

The disciples came up empty-handed after a "hard day's night" of fishing, too.

They had dragged their net up and down the waters of the sea all night – but for naught. Time after time, their net came up empty. No fish. No luck. Or so they thought. That is until Jesus came.

"Throw your net over on the other side of the boat and you will catch some," He called to the disheartened disciples. Obediently, they did so, and soon they could not haul in the net for the multitude of shiny, silver fishes.

When the disciples disembarked on land, Jesus had a charcoal fire burning, ready to bake some of the fresh fish. "Come and have breakfast," He invited. The chill and disappointment of the night were dispelled by the presence of the Living Lord, and by the bread and fish for their hungry stomachs (see John 21 for details).

Disappointment. You know what it's all about. Your long sought after dream has gone up in smoke. You've given it your best only to pull up a dripping line and some tangled weeds. Like some people I've talked to:

- A wife who has given a marriage everything she had, only to find that her husband has been unfaithful and has left her dangling emotionally and financially. Devastated.

- A couple near the goal of retirement. But the doctor's latest prognosis gave reason for distress not anticipation. Surgery. A restrictive lifestyle. Inactivity not productivity in the golden years.

- A manager in a large company who was a model executive. Called in and handed the pink slip. Position terminated.

- A student who burned the midnight oil to study and prepare. But the test results are below entrance requirements. The door of opportunity is slammed in his face.

- A defensive end on the high school football team, preparing all season for the finals... only to suffer the disappointment of a twisted ankle just before the big game.

"That's it! I'm tossing in the towel!" That's our natural reaction.

Lift your eyes just beyond the misty shore, and you will see the glowing embers of hope. A charcoal fire on the sand. Nourishment. Warm fellowship. A Saviour who cares. New horizons.

As we reach out to Jesus, reassurance returns and we can face the world with dignity.

🦑 GROWING RICH

John 21; Psalm 40

🔖 INVESTING WISELY

Facing disappointment? Learn from John 21.

1. BE ENCOURAGED. *If the living Jesus appeared to a boat full of disappointed fishermen, He will also come near to me in the hour of my need.*

2. BE CONFIDENT. *Jesus knows more about my struggle than I know. He knows where the school of fish is hiding, and He will make them available at just the right time.*

3. BE GRATEFUL. *The Lord who feeds cold, hungry fishermen will also provide for me in my hour of disappointment. He'll send a Gord to hand me a string of trout!*

6
Bats

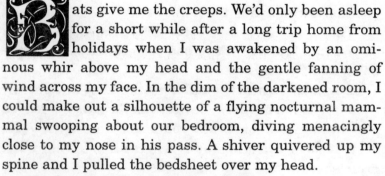ats give me the creeps. We'd only been asleep for a short while after a long trip home from holidays when I was awakened by an ominous whir above my head and the gentle fanning of wind across my face. In the dim of the darkened room, I could make out a silhouette of a flying nocturnal mammal swooping about our bedroom, diving menacingly close to my nose in his pass. A shiver quivered up my spine and I pulled the bedsheet over my head.

"Bat!" I shuddered. "Faye! Wake up!" I whispered hoarsely. "There's a bat in our room!"

Faye pulled the sheet over her head too.

We discussed strategy. Open outside door. Get broom. Chase bat out.

Cautiously, I peeked out from under the corner of the sheet. There he was all right. A naked bat hanging upside-down on the wall... just waiting for me to uncover my head.

This would call for valiant bravery – a dangerous leap for the door to fetch the broom. But who? Suddenly, the bed sheet shot to one side and a flying Faye made a frantic dash for the hallway. And she slammed the door behind her! I carefully re-adjusted the sheet around my ears. The bat was locked in the bedroom. Alone with me. Or so I thought.

"AAAAAAYEEEEOUUU! LAUUUURENNNNCE! HE'S OUT HEEEERE!"

Astonishingly, the bat had swooped a simultaneous escape with Faye's nightgown flurry and was making circuits up and down the hallway. I was safe (for the moment), but I had to rescue Faye!

Garnering pit bull courage, I volunteered combat position with Faye in the hall.

The outside door was open – Faye had done that.

We had brooms – Faye had seen to that. If only the bat would fly the coop.

But bats are nearly blind, I'm told. They navigate by radar. This bat's honing device was flawed. He dodged our swinging brooms, but could not detect the open door. Too bad! We desperately wanted him to vacate the premises.

All of sudden, his radar detected open air waves, and with one desperate dive, he was gone. Whew! This bravery stuff is exhausting! So why is Faye cool as a cucumber, while my heart is racing like a speedway?

Now, Faye says I've exaggerated some (I think it's all perspective!). But this is no exaggeration: There are preying powers and principalities swooping in upon us. Rulers of darkness. Spiritual wickedness in high places. Demonic authority. We wrestle against an entire army of invisible wicked spirits here on earth (see Ephesians 6:13) – spiritual forces fighting against God in schools, across radio waves, via television satellites and in magazine racks. Like vampire bats, they seek an entrance to our homes and hearts. Their goal is simple: Destroy our morality and families, our integrity and reputation.

Hiding under covers won't protect us. Running won't isolate us. Even a brave wife with broom in hand cannot ward off the attacks of this insidious enemy. Since we are fighting spirit powers, we need spiritual equipment – God's armour:

- the belt of honesty to hold our life together with a clear conscience.

- the breastplate of right living that annuls false accusations.

- sandals that carry the Good News that God loves us.

- a faith shield that douses flaming darts of temptation.

- the helmet of salvation that knows beyond a shadow of a doubt that we belong to God.

- and the Spirit's sword which is God's Word to strike back when the enemy pounces.

We blocked the chimney to keep out the winged bat, but no ordinary weapon will keep away wicked principalities. Only God's armour will do.

🦇 GROWING RICH

Ephesians 6:10-20

🦙 INVESTING WISELY

Try this experiment for one week:

Determine to match time watching T.V. with an equal time of Bible reading and prayerful meditating. (Average daily TV viewing per household: more than 7 hours!)

7
A Word From Home

o matter how the crow flies, it's a long way from Brockville, Canada, to Tema, West Africa. A long way!

At the moment, I'm seated under a palm tree, a cool glass of bitter lemon in hand, and I'm thousands of miles from the frosty chills of Canada. The mid-winter African sun beams warmly overhead and the forecast calls for blue skies ahead. A gentle breeze teases the long sprays of pink and violet bougainvillaea cascading across the protective fence that separates our mission house from the dusty outer street.

A piece of paradise? You bet! Shangri La? Close to it! Except for one thing. It's my birthday and all those near and dear are far away. Of course, I'm not pouting, nor am I feeling sorry for myself (I've preached sermons about that sort of thing). It's just that as more years "tick by," the more consolation I appreciate from those who "stick by" while hair fades and stomach falls.

Brrrrring. Brrrrring. The telephone. I do a quick time zone calculation. Eleven minus five. Yes! Six a.m. in Brockville. Faye's alarm has sounded to rise and

31

shine, and she has dialed from Canada to wish me a Happy Birthday. At least that's my guess.

"Hello! Hello! Helloooo!" Pastor Joe from the mission centre shouts valiantly into the receiver, but no gentle Faye-like voice bubbles back across the line to ask for me. Just static and booming wind.

"Faye," his voice calls in desperation, "I can't hear you. Hang up and dial again."

Click. We stare at the phone and wait. But the phone only stares back in stark silence. And because of Ghana's infamous telephone lines, I cannot return the call.

There's nothing like the sound of the voice of someone you love when you are a long way from home. It's assuring. Affirming. Consoling. Not to make decisions. Not to resolve conflict. Not to solve problems. Simply to talk and hear those words, "I love you and miss you a lot." It's the anticipation of completing my mission, ultimately stepping off the airbus into waiting hugs and kisses... and being home.

I can handle being on a mission as long as I can get a word from home now and again. Jesus could too. He needed moments with the Father who could understand and encourage Him. That's why we read that Jesus would withdraw up to a mountain. Early in the morning, the Lord would find His inner strength renewed by a word from the Father.

The world was pounding at His door. Clamouring for His attention. Jesus withdrew to the solitude of His Father's voice.

All of us need to withdraw to a place of solitude to hear the voice of God. To get a word from Home now and again. To be reassured and reaffirmed.

C. Austin Miles understood this when he wrote, "And He walks with me, and He talks with me, and He tells me I am His own. And the joy we share as we tarry there, none other has ever known."

By the way, I did have a wonderful birthday. Pastor Joe's wife, Jemima, baked a scrumptious chocolate chip birthday cake and put a musical candle on a pineapple (the candle wouldn't quit playing "Happy Birthday," so we submerged it in a cup of water – music still bubbled to the top!). There were gifts: an African shirt and a tape of African music. And my mother did get through from Canada later in the day... said it was -24°C, and wished me Happy Birthday.

But most special of all was a birthday card in my suitcase:

Dear Laurence,

This is your basic Birthday Card!
It doesn't have a computer chip in it that plays a
romantic ballad...
Why did I buy it? I guess the message inside caught
my eye...
I love you. I wish you "warm" birthday greetings.
I am grateful God has given us all these birthdays
together.
When you return, we will do a "birthday lunch" –
a date day!
Thinking of you often.

Love always,
Faye XOX

A word from the one I love. I could hardly wait!

&❧ GROWING RICH

Luke 9:28-35

&❧ INVESTING WISELY

Get alone with your Bible. Find a place of solitude. Read slowly and prayerfully until you HEAR God speaking. His voice is often still and small, not loud and brash... sometimes a gentle whisper. You may hear a word of encouragement. Perhaps a word of instruction. A quiet word of hope. You need to hear a word from the Father now and then. It keeps your spirits up when you're a long way from home.

8
Diamond Anniversary

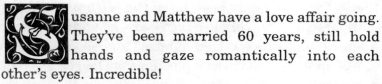usanne and Matthew have a love affair going. They've been married 60 years, still hold hands and gaze romantically into each other's eyes. Incredible!

In 1954, Susanne and Matthew Smallegange left their home in Holland for the prospects of beginning anew in Canada. The hardships of war had devastated the Dutch economy. So Matthew and Susanne gathered their few belongings into suitcases, took their ten children by the hand and immigrated to Canada to start over. They ultimately settled on a farm near Mallorytown, Ontario.

It was a family farm from the start. Eight daughters and two sons shared the choring, gardening, planting and harvesting. After each evening meal, Matthew opened the Bible and read to the family. One of his favourite readings was Psalm 90:1-2:

Lord, thou hast been our dwelling place
in all generations.
Before the mountains were brought forth,
or ever thou hadst formed the earth and the world,
even from everlasting to everlasting, thou art God.

On Saturday and Sunday evenings, the family gathered in the living room for hymn sings. They were the old Dutch hymns from Holland. But as English became more proficient, Susanne could be heard leading the family chorus: "Grace, grace, God's grace. Grace that will pardon and cleanse within... Grace that is greater than all our sin."

After 60 years of marriage, you don't need to ask Matthew and Susanne what they think about home and family. You need only peek in on the celebration in the church hall. The Smalleganges are celebrating their diamond anniversary. One hundred and eleven descendants applaud their accomplishment. The elderly pair beam with joy. And there is good reason for the old Dutch couple to rejoice. Not only have they lived to a good ripe age, but not one of the Smallegange family has given in to divorce or separation. Could it have something to do with the old family Bible? The family thinks so, because they had it rebound and presented to Mom and Dad as a memento to their years of spiritual leadership.

Sixty years of marriage, living with the same person! There are memories that linger. Precious memories. Funny memories. Painful memories. All drip with nostalgia and reminiscence.

The celebration concludes with a hymn sing. One is sung in Dutch, which grandchildren and great grandchildren barely mouth. Baby Shane, the youngest, only coos. Finally, there is a mighty chorus: "Praise God From Whom All Blessings Flow." It rises to a crescendo, the climax of the day. It was meant to be the finale, but Susanne continues. This is a moment to savour. Possess. Cling to. Leaning on her walker, chin tilted with resolute determination, the old matriarch sings her final testimony: "God is so good, He's so good to me." It's like a farewell address – a testimony of God's faithfulness throughout the years, and a challenge to one hundred and eleven descendants to keep the faith.

A holy hush hangs across the hall when the last note is sung. Matthew and Susanne hug and kiss. It's the stuff of roots and family traditions. And memories.

There will never be a Smallegange reunion like this again. Unless in heaven. And I'd like to peek in on that great celebration too. To see Matthew and Susanne hug and kiss. Hear their family sing around the Throne: "Great and marvelous are Thy works, Lord God Almighty."

Until that day, may the Smallegange circle be unbroken! Yours too. And mine.

GROWING RICH

The Book of Ruth

INVESTING WISELY

Plan a family celebration. Keep it simple. Pop some popcorn. Share some cake. Use the opportunity to express one thing you appreciate about each member. Hold hands and pray.

9
Angel Unawares

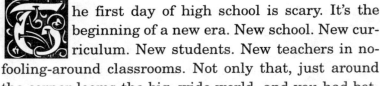he first day of high school is scary. It's the beginning of a new era. New school. New curriculum. New students. New teachers in no-fooling-around classrooms. Not only that, just around the corner looms the big, wide world, and you had better take your studies seriously if you ever hope to get a job, enter a career and make your way in life.

My high school began in Grade 10 at Newbrook High. Our high school was very small. In fact, our total enrollment in Grade 10 was only ten!

But the most exciting event for us on September 1st was the new teacher who would be teaching most of our senior matric subjects. Her name was Miss White, a pretty blonde, fresh out of university, and only about four years older than her new Grade 10 class. She was also the daughter of the local pastor from the little Pentecostal Church, situated next door to the school. Miss White had the aura of an angel.

How fortunate we were to have Miss White as our teacher. She was an instructor "par excellence." To her, I credit my foundations in math and science that carried me through the following two years of senior matriculation.

And what a year we had with Miss White! Yes, we had rules for classroom behaviour and homework completion. But they were unspoken. I remember our principal announcing over the intercom that we were to address our new teacher as "Miss White" (and not as "Madeline," as some knew her.) But Mr. Sidor might have saved his breath, for he need not have legislated respect as far as we were concerned. Room 10 loved Miss White, and we worked our fingers to the bone for her. No one dared disappoint her. Her disciplinary action consisted of a sorrowful look that pierced our young hearts with remorse and contrition.

I thought of Miss White while reading Seven Things God Hates (Prov. 6: 16-19). The title sounds so stern and strict... severe. But it's not. These seven qualities actually break the heart of God... like we thought Miss White's heart would break should we fail or disappoint her. That's why God hates them. These attitudes and behaviours unleash a volley of grief and misery upon innocent children, rip apart homes and families, maim bodies of young men and women, and obliterate towns and cities in war. God hates them because God is love. He loves us too much to stand by and watch without emotion when we demonstrate the character flaws that cause such pain and sorrow.

So, when you really love God, you won't want to break His heart. You will want to please Him, like we wanted to please Miss White. You are convinced that God, like our Grade 10 teacher, has your best interest at heart.

Take a moment to review the list of Seven Things from Proverbs 6 that break God's heart. Contrast them with the Seven Things from Matthew 5 (the Beatitudes) that bring God joy:

1. God hates PRIDE that says, "I don't need God," but loves HUMILITY that admits need.

2. God hates LYING to cover up dishonesty, but loves TRUTHFULNESS at all costs.

3. God hates VIOLENCE that harms, but loves QUIETNESS and KINDNESS.

4. God hates EVIL PLOTS to get the better of someone, but loves PURE THOUGHTS that hunger after right living.

5. God hates EAGERNESS TO DO WRONG – enthusiasm to bring pain to others – but loves MERCY and KINDNESS.

6. God hates HYPOCRISY (living a lie), but loves HONESTY that admits weakness and failure.

7. God hates SOWING DISCORD, but loves words of ENCOURAGEMENT and EDIFICATION.

Jesus said that you may not be the most popular person in the world if you live like this. But one thing is certain: You'll pass the grade with God! And He in turn will bless you.

๛ GROWING RICH

Proverbs 6:16-19; Matthew 5:1-16

🐾 INVESTING WISELY

Write a note of appreciation to a teacher who especially helped you during your years of schooling. That teacher will be ecstatic. I plan to send this story to Miss White!

10
Starting Over

Last night I couldn't get my act together! It was one of those "Ladies Night Out" dessert and coffee hours that our church sponsors, and I was billed as the guest singer. Elegant waiters, attired in flaming red cummerbunds and matching bow ties whisked about with noiseless efficiency, pouring coffee and serving sweet dainties. Crafts and holiday decorations adorned the large banquet hall.

I was first on the program. The master of ceremonies gave me an enthusiastic introduction. "Would you please welcome our pastor as he comes to sing tonight." Applause filled the auditorium.

I stepped up to the microphone and nodded to the sound engineer. The sound track began on cue with the beautiful orchestral introduction of my song. But I couldn't hear the music beat. It was too faint. I panicked. I tried to sing along but the orchestra was playing the chorus, and I was still singing the verse.

The engineer stopped the tape. I mumbled an apology. The ladies clapped politely.

We started again. Same problem. I still couldn't hear the back-up tape well enough to stay in sync.

There I was – pastor, author, guest singer – in front of an auditorium filled with ladies and I couldn't sing with that tape. I felt like a fool. I wanted to sit down and hide my head under one of the fine linen tablecloths.

So what do you do? Sit down in frustration? Or try again? I decided to try once more. I asked the ladies to be patient. I instructed the engineer to make some adjustments... and turn up the volume.

Soon the elegant sound of violins and cellos filled the banquet hall. I could hear. I was on track. I began to sing along without a hitch.

Starting over is not easy. Our natural reaction is to quit... to give up... to hide in the crowd. We're embarrassed. Humiliated. Our dignity is damaged. We've fallen flat on our pride.

But would you believe that one of our favourite Bible books was written by someone who quit, and then started over again? His name was John Mark, and he wrote the Gospel of Mark. Half way through his first missionary journey with the Apostle Paul and Uncle Barnabas, John Mark quit and returned home. When it came time to plan a second trip, Barnabas was willing to give John Mark a second chance, but not Paul. So Barnabas took John and sailed for Cyprus. Whatever Paul observed as weakness in Mark at this point was later overcome. Mark triumphed over his weakness. He didn't quit. He started over. Paul was so impressed, he later changed his tune about the young man and commended Mark's efforts in ministry (2 Tim. 4:11).

God uses people who start over. The Halls of Faith are lined with their names. John Mark was one. His doggedness compelled him to write the innumerable eyewitness accounts of Jesus. You and I are benefiting from that today.

Perhaps you feel like quitting as you read this today. You've stumbled... made a fool of yourself... let someone down... erred... opened your mouth when you should have kept it closed. You're miserable and feel like a failure. You'd like to hide in some closet.

But don't give in to self pity, despair or discouragement. Quitters are a dime a dozen. Get back up. Move on. Breathe in the fresh promises of encouragement from God's Word.

Get your second wind and start over again. You'll be glad you did!

🐾 GROWING RICH

1. *Acts 13:13; 15:35-41*

2. *Set a goal during the next few days to read the entire Gospel of Mark. Keep in mind that Mark became a close associate of Peter. Tradition refers to Mark's work as the memoirs of Peter. As you read, picture the younger disciple, Mark, feeling compelled to write these eyewitness accounts for the benefit of future generations.*

🐾 INVESTING WISELY

Be a Barnabas this week. Reach out to someone who is discouraged. Empathize. Encourage them to try one more time.

11
Growing Strong

big oak tree grows smack-dab in the middle of our parking lot. Three hundred years of growth and strength... twisted by winds, scarred by saws, chewed by insects and pecked by birds.

I have a deep affection for that old tree. Every spring this stately giant opens an umbrella of leafy spring shade... volunteers a strong arm for a summer swing... scatters acorns for skittish squirrels... stands on guard to meet the onslaught of winter's wind.

On occasion, I've gone out and put my arms around the gnarled trunk of my ancient friend. I can reach less than halfway around, but I want to hug the old tree for being there – for being strong, steadfast and stable, flourishing in good seasons, and holding on in bad. I respect this old oak tree for its age, yes, but more for taking whatever is thrown at it. It doesn't matter what storms blow or how hot the sun beats – no matter what, in drought, heat and cold, this tree has stood its ground. I can always count on the oak tree to stand firm. That's because there are roots reaching beneath the rocks for water, nutrients, and support. The leaves and acorns are signs of life in that tree.

The writer of Psalm 1 describes a man who resembles the old oak in our parking lot. He is a godly man who delights in the Word of God; who meditates day and night on what God's Word means for his life.

He shall be like a tree planted by the rivers of water,
That brings forth his fruit in his season;
His leaf also shall not wither;
And whatsoever he does shall prosper.

The apostle Paul also knew the need for deep roots. He prayed that the energetic Ephesian believers would be "rooted and grounded in love" (Eph. 3:17). And the wise apostle urged the Colossian Christians to be "rooted and built up... and established in the faith" (Col. 2:7). Paul knew these young believers needed to sink strong roots deep into the rock of God's Word. Paul was most anxious that they grow strong and stable, and not wither with the advent of tough times and adversity.

I'd like my life to be like the oak in our parking lot. Strong, stately, stable – not fickle like blowing chaff. But to be a strong oak, I need a sturdy network of spreading roots.

I must remember: Deep roots take time, discipline and persistence. I must not expect someone to pat me on the back and say, "My! What fine roots you are developing!" Strong roots grow over the long haul – away from public applause and in the privacy of God's Word. They mature in a quiet place... some upper attic or private closet... some threadbare chair. Daily, I search for spiritual responses to life. My understanding of biblical insights is broadened. My faith is stretched with examples of God's faithfulness.

The fruit that I bear is a sign of life in me.

Don't dare cut down my oak tree! Drop by and admire it. Park your car under it. Yes, even take a picture, if you wish. But please leave the aged friend as my object lesson and inspiration to grow deeply into God and His Word.

🐾 GROWING RICH

Psalm 1; Matthew 13:3-23; Ephesians 3:7-4:3; Colossians 2:6-3:4

🐾 INVESTING WISELY

1. *Memorize Psalm 1 this week.*

2. *Mark a day on your calendar. Set aside a solid hour to simply read your Bible. Choose a New Testament letter. Make notes. Ask God to incorporate insights into your character and life.*

12
Refinished Antiques

he baker's cupboard was a hundred years old and looked it. Wrinkled paint could no longer hide the scuffs and stains that had accumulated over the years from punching bread dough, slopping pickle juice and spilling wild raspberry jam. Once the focal point of a busy home, the sad old relic now tottered in a forlorn corner of our neighbour's musty back shed. Rejected and demoted, the old hoosier was more a candidate for kindling than a cupboard for our kitchen.

But Faye's eyes misted wistfully. "It's like Grandma Montgomery's," she whispered. A kaleidoscope of memories danced through her mind: hot baked bread, buttered and sprinkled with melting brown sugar and cinnamon; a kindly, silver-haired grandma bustling about with flour on her nose; snowy winter nights spent snuggled up on Grandma's rocking chair across from the crackling wood stove. Warmth. Security. Love.

"I'd like to have that cupboard," she said to the owner. And before my pragmatic nature could object, Faye had purchased Grandma's Kitchen Centre for $75.

Suffice it to say, weeks of tedious scraping, sanding and filling were required to restore the ancient cabinet to respectable kitchen status. But I'm proud to report that no longer does the old baker sadly droop in the dusty shed. Instead, she has taken proud residence in our kitchen – a work of historic authenticity and pride. Pioneer kitchen utensils are displayed on her shelves, and visitors ask where we found such an intriguing piece of antiquity.

The old cupboard is a spiritual parable. God finds us in a sad state of brokenness and disrepair. We were lost in some dusty corner of disrepute and disgrace. He places us on the carpenter bench of life to restore in us the character of His Son, Jesus Christ.

There is sanding and scraping:

- Irritations to redirect our thoughts.
- Losses to refocus our goals.
- Reverses to reduce our self-sufficiency.

So how should we react to the process?

Four steps must be followed in this refinishing process to transform an old junker into a sparkling jewel:

1. RESPOND with a positive outlook – praise.

James says, "Count it all joy." Realize God uses various trials to test our faith and produce in us mature character – like it was before it was marred and scuffed by sin (see James 1:2-4).

2. REBUILD thought structures by reading and memorizing Scripture.

Learn to think like God thinks... see how He sees.

3. REFOCUS for the future.

Picture what God is planning to do for your life. Understand that the end product will be admired and valued.

4. REPRODUCE your life.

Share the process with others. You're believable and others will listen.

GROWING RICH

James 1

INVESTING WISELY

My greatest trial at present is _____.

1. I am responding with praise by _____.

2. I am rebuilding my thought structure by _____

    _____.

3. I believe God wants me to become (character quality)

    _____.

4. I will share what I learned with _____.

Congratulations! You are moving from the dusty garage to the hub of living. God's kitchen is full of good things.

13

Broncobusting

y cousin, Delvin, has a most unusual hobby. Broncobusting. Last Christmas, he explained to me the fine art of riding a snorting, contorting rodeo bronco, should I ever take up the notion.

The first challenge is to mount the squirming beast (easier said than done!). Ready? Give the nod. Open the chute and release the brute into the main arena.

Now, the fun begins. The first action is to run spurs up and down the flank of the nasty hombre – apparently to encourage him to buck. In the meantime, your body must synchronize to the rhythm of the rock 'n roll. Oh, yes, rules say, no hanging on for dear life with two hands – only one. The other must wave frantically in the air. Losing your Stetson adds to the drama. Hopefully, you will remain in the saddle long enough to hear the eight-second buzzer at which time you attempt to dismount without getting kicked in the head with flying hooves. Now, pick up your hat. Dust off your chaps. And acknowledge the cheers of the grandstand crowd.

Only in the wild west!

Rodeo broncos are never broken to ride. They always buck. Their behavior is never controlled. But other horses can be mastered. Colts can be taught to lead with a special bit placed in their mouths. It may take an hour, or it may take half a day, but once the colt is mastered, he never forgets. He will always lead... always be under control.

Bucking broncos are not pictures of spirit-filled Christians. God desires to lead us gently by His Spirit. A Spirit-filled believer doesn't buck, but is led. The Holy Spirit gives power to exercise self-control, and, at the same time, leads us in God's will.

Paul explains these truths in 1 Corinthians 6:

1. SELF-CONTROL: Learning to take the wrong, even when in the right.

    "All things are lawful unto me (I can do anything I want to), but all things are not expedient (helpful): all things are lawful for me, but I will not be brought under the power of any" (vs. 12).

Paul speaks to his Corinthian friends and says, "Why do you not rather take the wrong... suffer yourself to be defrauded?"

Jesus calls it turning the other cheek... going the second mile (Matt. 5:38-42).

2. HOLY SPIRIT CONTROL: Disciplining my appetites because my body is God's dwelling place.

    "What? Do you not know that your body is the temple of the Holy Spirit, which is in you, which you have of God, and you are not your own?" (vs. 19).

Ever visit a new building site? What a mess! The place is littered with sawdust, soft drink cans, cardboard boxes and scraps of lumber and shingles. But when the new owner moves in, the trash is cleaned up. Everything is spic and span. The new owner wants the house to be clean and presentable. His house is a testimony to his reputation.

Now your body houses a new Owner. The Holy Spirit lives in you (vs. 19). And when the Holy Spirit lives in you, He gives the self-control to clean up your "housekeeping act" (see vs. 9-11).

Delvin aroused my curiosity. One hot summer day, I found myself sitting in the stands of the Ponoka Stampede. I stretched my neck to watch the bucking broncos preparing for action. The rodeo hands gave them little attention except to crack long ropes and herd these untamed horses into a corral.

Then came the riding ponies. What a difference! They were under the control of a rider and received special treatment. They were combed. Curried. Decked out with fancy blankets and saddles. They pranced proudly under the reins of pretty cowgirls and handsome cowboys. The crowd applauded.

Similarly, Paul emphasizes, "Do you not know that the wicked will not inherit the kingdom of God?" He tells why by listing a catalogue of sins that would make the Cisco Kid blush – unmanageable, uncontrolled, undisciplined – like a bronco seeking his own way.

But not those who belong to God. "You were washed, sanctified, justified in the name of the Lord Jesus and by the Spirit of our God" (vs. 12). You are God's special, set-aside people under the control of God's Spirit!

Think it over. Better to be led by the Spirit than to spend your life kicking against the spurs!

🐾 GROWING RICH

1 Corinthians 6; Matthew 5:38-42; Acts 26

🐾 INVESTING WISELY

Prayerfully consider:

- *When wronged, do I bristle? Jump to defend myself?*

- *When hurt, do I desire to get back... even the score?*

- *Am I abrasive... like sandpaper, always rubbing others the wrong way?*

- *Do I carry a spiritual chip on my shoulder, an "I've been hurt" attitude?*

- *Am I disciplined in my habits? Am I a slave to an undesirable appetite?*

14
Sight With No Vision

elen Keller, blind and deaf from infancy, was once asked, "Is there anything worse than blindness?"

"Oh, yes!" she responded. "A person with sight and no vision."

History reminds us that those who have most influenced their generation for God have been those inflamed by a vision. The halls of faith are inscribed with the names of risk-takers who were not known for playing it safe. Invariably, they were motivated by a mission in life – a purpose, a possibility, a goal which looked beyond the mundane to a dream bigger than themselves.

The Apostle Paul was one of such vision. In Acts 16, we read that a man of Macedonia (northern Greece) called to him, "Come over and help us." There is good reason to believe this man was none other than Dr. Luke.

Picture that late night scene. Luke and Paul are pouring over a tattered sheepskin map of Greece. A flickering candle illuminates their intense faces. Luke's appeal is convincing:

- Open doors are before us;
- Travel is accessible;
- There is hunger for spiritual reality.

The next thing we know, Paul has his bags packed with a ticket in his hand for Macedonia. First stop: Philippi. No red carpet welcome there. Just a few women praying near the river. A short while later, Paul and Silas have their shirts stripped, and a brutal Roman whip is tearing at their backs. A pagan jailer locks them up and puts their feet in stocks. But Paul's determination is not crushed. A small church begins to flourish in the home of Lydia, the business woman. Soon Paul and his companions are trudging along the Via Egnatia, enroute to the capital, Thessalonica. Berea, Athens and Corinth are next on the itinerary. More imprisonment. Hardship. Uproars.

But the passion of a vision compels Paul onward until he exclaims: "I must also see Rome!" (Acts 19:21). Rome is the strategic centre of the world. All roads lead to Rome. These highways will be God's highways – arteries along which messengers of the Gospel might wend their way to every corner of the world.

That flaming torch of vision has been passed on to countless others:

- David Livingston, Bible in hand, marched through the uncharted jungles of Africa. He faced countless dangers and unbelievable difficulties. His zeal was spurred on by the cruelty of the slave trade, and he became determined to crush what he called "the open sore of the world."

VISION fires our determination to invest in a worthwhile mission.

- Hudson Taylor, the sickly bank accountant, became God's venturer and the first missionary to China's interior. His contagious faith and fervor influenced countless others to lives of extraordinary service.

VISION sees beyond the majority and inspires others to follow.

- Fanny Crosby was only six weeks old when she became permanently blinded. Her mother explained to her that God sometimes takes away one gift in order to give a better one. In this way, Fanny was never bitter about her blindness, and at eight years of age, wrote:

  > *How many blessings I enjoy,*
  > *That other people don't.*
  > *To weep and sigh because I'm blind,*
  > *I cannot, and I won't.*

Many of the best known songs and hymns used in our churches today were written by Fanny J. Crosby.

VISION is not thwarted by personal handicaps and self-pity.

A vision will change your life. So, lift up your sights. Look beyond your own little puddle to see new potential... new possibilities... new perimeters. Be all you can be. Reach to new heights. It's God's will.

Don't settle for less than the best.

﹩ GROWING RICH

Genesis 12:1-9; Acts 16:6-34

﹩ INVESTING WISELY

1. *Be courageous. Write down your dream. Ask God for wisdom. Explore every possible avenue to make your dream come true.*

2. *Extend a helping hand to someone in need. Worthwhile visions always involve meeting the needs of others.*

15
Mystery Talk at Easter

teenager's room is a mystery! At least that's what Fred and I concluded over lunch the other day. And we should know. We both have teenagers.

A teenager can enter a perfectly tidy bedroom, walk out 30 minutes later, and it resembles a hurricane disaster zone. It's a mystery to me.

But that's not the only mystery I can't explain.

Why does toast always land peanut butter side down on the floor – never right side up?

There's the mystery of the universe: Some of the stars twinkling in the sky have ceased to be millions of years ago... and I can still see them. Incredible!

What about the tiny seed that germinates and grows into an orange, carrot or red beet?

And there is the mystery of a mother's soothing hand on a little boy's fevered brow.

The mystery of birth, aging and death.

Life is full of unexplainable riddles... unsolvable puzzles... mysteries. We scratch our heads and wonder why. So is it any wonder God's Word contains some mystery talk? Some unexplainable truths which defy understanding?

It's that way with Easter. Who can understand how Jesus could rise from the dead? Certainly the disciples were the first to express their unbelief that Jesus had risen. Thomas shook his head and said, "Unless I see the nail prints and the sword wound, I won't believe."

Paul writes that there is no denying the great mystery of godliness (1 Tim. 3:16). He continues by listing six pillars of profession that make the Christian faith unique. He does so by quoting one of the hymns of the early church – a chant which believers recited to reaffirm their basic beliefs:

1. There is the MYSTERY OF CHRISTMAS: God appeared in human body.

2. There is the MYSTERY OF EASTER: Jesus proved Himself alive.

3. There is the MYSTERY OF ANGELS: He was seen by angels.

4. There is the MYSTERY OF THE CHURCH: Believers are found throughout the world in every culture.

5. There is the MYSTERY OF THE ASCENSION: Jesus was received up into heaven.

Easter reminds us of God's mysterious power. Through the power of the Spirit, Jesus came back to life. The empty tomb is a mystery! It proved Jesus to be all He claimed to be.

O, the wonder of it all! I don't understand it. It's a mystery.

But I believe it!

❧ GROWING RICH

1 Corinthians 15

❧ INVESTING WISELY

Share this object lesson with a small child:

Plant a (bean) seed in a small pot of soil. Print the words of 1 Corinthians 15:20 on the label. Water and watch it grow.

16

Harvest Time

ou can take the boy out of the country, but you can't take the country out of the boy. It's true, because I'm one of them. I get "country pangs" every fall at harvest time.

Harvesting in my boyhood days involved everyone in the family plus nearby neighbours. We had our own grain binder, so Dad and I spent the month of August cutting and stooking the grain for drying. But when threshing time rolled around in September, more help was needed, so we joined forces with nearby relatives and friends. It seemed as if our entire fall was crammed into those four frantic weeks. Teams of horses hauled huge wagon loads of bundles in a continuous stream to the chomping jaws of the monster threshing machine.

Uncle Bill was my favourite teamster. He would arrive early in the morning and you could hear his clear, melodious whistle above the rattle of his rack and wagon and the snorting of his team of horses. His horses were muzzled to keep them from feeding while being led from stook to stook. Sometimes they barely paused as the bundles came flying up on the wagon to be stacked in precise rows for transport to the thresher.

The threshing machine was a fascination. It was powered by a snorting Model-D John Deere tractor, its big rubber wheels braced with wooden blocks to keep the flapping drive-belt taut. The sheaves were pitched into the feeder and rode unsuspectingly along the moving slats until they were suddenly slashed by vicious teeth and shaken apart. My job was to shovel back the grain that poured down the spout into the dust granary. On occasion, Uncle Walter would let me raise the rumbling blower which belched billowing clouds of straw and chaff into an ever-mounting golden stack.

Evening was the climax of the day. As darkness settled, horses were watered, tied to a rail fence and fed oat bundles. The harvesters made their way into the house and washed their hands in a basin. Soon they settled around the gas lit kitchen table which groaned with platters of roast beef, bowls of mashed potatoes and turnips, corn, rich brown gravy and heaping plates of fresh buns and butter. Just when you thought you couldn't eat another crumb, in would come homemade pies: apple, lemon meringue, pumpkin and chocolate loaded with whipped cream. Steaming mugs of hot tea and boiled coffee helped wash the feast down.

SPIRITUAL HARVEST

A follower of Jesus can't get harvest time out of his heart either. When Jesus went about all the cities and villages, preaching and healing, He saw the great multitudes and was moved with compassion. He saw that they fainted and were scattered like sheep without a shepherd. Then He said to His disciples, "The harvest is truly plenteous, but the threshers are few. Pray that the Lord of the harvest will send forth threshers into His harvest" (paraphrase of Matthew 9:35-38).

Yes, the harvest is ripe before us – multitudes are everywhere. I see them when I walk into a teeming mall. I think of them when I roar off in a giant aircraft over a throbbing city. And I rub elbows with them everyday:

- the school chums of my kids;
- a grieving staff person at work;
- the parents of my Grade 5 students;
- a clerk at the store;
- the clients that I service.

Where are the harvesters? Those moved with compassion? Who will help gather in the harvest?

Let us pray for labourers. Let us work together like the harvesters of yesteryear. Some will plant, others water, and some will harvest the golden grain. And when it's time to tie up the harvest rack at the "Pearly Gates," we'll be ready to sit down to that great feast with Jesus, prepared by God for His great "threshing crew."

I can almost hear Uncle Bill's whistle now.

GROWING RICH

Matthew 9:35-10:42

INVESTING WISELY

1. *Volunteer to help in your church youth program or Sunday School hour.*

2. *Build a bridge to someone who needs God. Make it a goal to share your faith.*

17

Run With Horses

ough men are products of tough times. Kites rise against the wind, not with it. Callus grows from hard work, not easy living. And when God wants to educate a man, He does not send him to the school of good times, but to the school of hard places:

- Joseph came to the throne of Egypt via the pit and prison.

- Moses tended sheep in the desert before leading a nation to freedom.

- Elijah sat by the drying brook before confronting the prophets of Baal.

- John Bunyan wrote *Pilgrim's Progress* in jail.

- Martin Luther translated the Bible while confined in the castle of Wartburg.

Jeremiah had to learn this lesson. He was worn down by opposition and ridicule, and absorbed in self-pity. His own townspeople hatched a plot to take his life.

For a moment we are not certain if Jeremiah will stand.
Will he retreat into a shell? Fade away into the mundane? Settle for being nothing more than a Jerusalem
statistic?

God bends over and whispers into Jeremiah's ear:
"If racing with footmen has wearied you, how will you
race against horses? And if you are frightened and
weary in a peaceful quiet land, how will you survive
in the jungle and flooding of Jordan?" (paraphrase of
Jeremiah 12:5).

Jeremiah was weary, haunted by fear. But he had
only run with footmen. At the critical moment, God
speaks: "Life is difficult, Jeremiah. But I've been getting you in shape for the big race... for the tough times
when you will need strong, spiritual muscle and fibre.
Are you going to quit at the drop of a pin? At the first
hint of difficulty? Will you retreat when the going gets
tough? Are you more interested in keeping your feet
dry, eating three square meals a day, getting eight
hours of sleep in a warm bed than living on the cutting
edge of risk for God's glory?

"Tell me, Jeremiah. What do you really want for
your life? Mediocrity or excellence? Run-of-the-mill
or achievement? Shuffling along with the crowd or
influence?"

Jeremiah contemplated his response. He had ren-
dered difficult service, but it was during a time of com-
parative peace – the reign of Josiah. There was yet more
severe service awaiting him – standing alone in turbu-
lence and upheaval. Jeremiah would be called upon to
exercise his ministry, as it were, among the dangerous
thickets in the wilds of Jordan.

Great men and women of God have always come through difficult times and turned problems into spiritual growth and creative opportunities. They have learned how to pray, sacrifice and risk more than the ordinary person. They have also expected more from God than the ordinary person – and received it!

That is always God's method for choice servants. He continually prepares men and women for the big race, the difficult enterprise, the more strenuous service. First, we learn how to run with footmen. Our muscles become hardened – prepared for the more difficult task of running with horses... accomplishing the extraordinary... the heroic... the impossible.

Some friends of ours are involved in missionary bootcamp with New Tribes Missions. Missionary candidates learn how to live in the wilderness, construct a primitive shelter, make their own utensils and cope without luxuries. If a candidate cannot make it through bootcamp, how will he survive on the primitive banks of the Orinoco?

Proverbs 24:10 reminds us that "if you faint in the day of adversity, your strength is small." It means you are not in shape. Your muscles are flabby. You are not ready to run with horses.

Have you made up your mind? Will you live cautiously or courageously? Will you be mundane or exceptional? Will you live at ease or stretch to the limit?

Jeremiah weighed the options. He tossed the alternatives around in his mind. He counted the cost.

"I'll run with horses!" he decided.

His life was his answer.

🐎 GROWING RICH

1. *Use the Living Bible to read Jeremiah 12:1-6. Continue reading chapter 28 and note how the prophet's moods fluctuated under stress between confident faith and agony of spirit. Finally, read chapter 42 and see how Jeremiah's ministry is ultimately sought out. He is running with horses!*

2. *Read the entire book of Esther – the account of a woman who learned to run with horses.*

🐎 INVESTING WISELY

Adopt this formula for success and "Run with Horses":

S – select a goal
U – unleash your spiritual gifts
C – commit the results to God
C – choose to glorify God
E – expect difficulties
S – stand firm, don't quit
S – surrender your life to Jesus Christ

18
A Woman Jesus Loved

er failure might have been fatal and her life might have been futile. Bitterness might have consumed her and resentment might have ruined her. Brenda's marriages had ended on the rocks, and she had received the ultimate death threat: cancer. Outwardly, she was a stunning beauty; inwardly, she was a muddled mess. In public, she was the life of the party; but in private, she was falling apart.

One Sunday, Brenda found herself in church. The worship was inspiring, the message was appealing, and Brenda took a faith step that would change the course of her life forever. She gave her life to Jesus Christ in a simple act of faith and trust. There was no hoopla, no thunder from the sky... just an act of commitment to the Saviour to take whatever was left of her life and make something good out of it. Jesus did!

For the next five years, Brenda worked on healing relationships. Want to hear about a miracle? She made friends with the wife of her former husband, the father of her two children. Was I dreaming, or was it an act of God? On Sunday, I would often see the two wives sitting together. They had become friends! I decided it was an act of God. Only God could pull off this sort of reconciliation.

Brenda made other friends – Christian friends. They laughed together. They met after church for brunch. They boarded a plane and soaked in the sun of Jamaica. They drank coffee at the donut shop and talked about spiritual things. They prayed together.

Everywhere Brenda went, she talked of how faith in God was sustaining her. She penned in her Bible: "Joy is that deep settled confidence that God is in control of every area of my life."

All the while, the deadly cancer was taking its course and eating away at her body. Radiation uprooted her hair. Brenda donned a wig, swallowed her nausea and clung to her faith. There were tears, prayers, anointing for healing. Brenda's heart was healed, but her body was deteriorating.

One day, I was called into the hospital to Brenda's room. I gasped inwardly at her frail body, hardly recognizable as the once vivacious woman with sharp wit and flashing eye. I grasped her hand and spoke softly to arouse her from sleep. She smiled weakly in recognition, and we quietly spoke of Jesus and His presence with us in the valley. Then I asked permission to sing Brenda's favourite song. The family gathered around in quiet reverence, and Brenda closed her eyes in worship.

> *Because He lives, I can face tomorrow;*
> *Because He lives, all fear is gone.* [1]

When I was done, there was a holy moment of silence, and Brenda opened her eyes. "You did well," she said, "but you could stand a little sharpening up, don't you think?" The hospital room erupted in laughter, and so did Brenda. I squeezed her hand and walked out with tears in my eyes, but joy in my heart.

Today, I preached Brenda's celebration service. Brenda wasn't there, only the remains of her body were placed in the sanctuary.

My thoughts were drawn to the life of Mary Magdalene. She too had been young and reckless. Lived in the fast lane. But her world fell apart and she was possessed by seven spirits that shackled her life and destroyed her peace. Until she met Jesus Christ! He loosened her from bondage, forgave her past and cleared up her bitterness. Mary was grateful. She joined a group of ladies who ministered to the practical needs of Jesus and His disciples while they plodded though the towns and villages, teaching and healing the masses (see Luke 8:2-3). Jesus loved Mary, and Mary loved Jesus – not romantically, but spiritually.

Mary was the first person to see Jesus alive after His death on the cross. She stood close by while soldiers nailed Jesus to the crossbeams, and she followed Joseph and Nicodemus while they laid Jesus in the tomb. Early Sunday morning, she made her way back to the tomb to minister to His body. The tomb was empty, as Jesus wasn't there. That's when Jesus revealed Himself to her, and she hurried away to tell the disciples and the world that Jesus was alive. She was never the same again.

Neither was Brenda! Before she fell asleep in death, she dictated a note to her children to be read at her funeral service:

Rob and Kristen:

You both have been the light of my life. I love you both more than you will ever know, and even more since you gave me three beautiful grandchildren.

Life hasn't always been easy for us, but with the love of God flowing through us, it has certainly mended many fences...

Always try to keep focused on the Lord. I know when I was your age, no one could tell me anything, but always remember this day is a celebration. I know that this is hard for you to understand, but please remember: no more pain, no more sickness... because today, I am with my loving Father and He has been with me through it all.

Again, do not doubt my love for you, and try not to be sad, because today I am dancing in heaven!

Love,
Mom.

🐾 GROWING RICH

John 20:1-18

🐾 INVESTING WISELY

Brenda's family requested that memorials to her life be given to "Love In Action," a practical ministry that helps the hurting, hungry and hopeless. Consider giving to a practical ministry that reaches out in compassion to the less fortunate. You may even hear Brenda's dance steps!

---

[1]Words by Gloria Gaither and William Gaither, 1971. Copyright (c) 1971 by William J. Gaither. All rights reserved.

19
Dad Handling

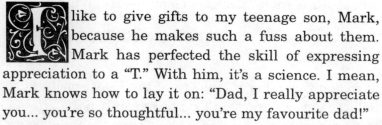like to give gifts to my teenage son, Mark, because he makes such a fuss about them. Mark has perfected the skill of expressing appreciation to a "T." With him, it's a science. I mean, Mark knows how to lay it on: "Dad, I really appreciate you... you're so thoughtful... you're my favourite dad!"

Mark knows I'm a sucker for his appreciative superlatives. He figures it softens me up for more of the same – makes me more vulnerable to continue showering him with privileges and favours. And he's right! It's called the "Psychology of Dad Handling."

Mark's recent Father's Day card expressed his philosophy perfectly:

> *Dad,*
>
> *How you've worked and slaved for me*
> *All these years!*
>
> *You've bought me pills,*
> *Big chief tablets, shoes, milk,*
> *Warm socks and teddy bears.*
>
> *When I think of the money you've spent*
> *On education, music lessons, paper clips...*

When I think of this,
I get all choked up
And can only say –

May it go on forever!

Happy Father's Day! [1]

Love, Mark

God loves to give to His children too! And the beautiful truth is this: There is no end to His giving.

1. God gives us the GIFT OF THE HOLY SPIRIT (Acts 2:33).

When God gives us the gift of the Holy Spirit, it can be likened to saying that God has given me the gift of a good wife. Faye is God's gift to me. From the moment we were married, I have enjoyed her love and loyalty... her friendship and fellowship... her care and consideration.

Likewise, the moment I accepted Jesus Christ as my Lord and Saviour, the Holy Spirit came to live within me in fellowship. He is God's gift to me because I am His child.

2. God gives us the FRUIT OF THE SPIRIT (Galatians 5:22, 23).

The fruit of the Spirit is inner character produced by the Holy Spirit in the life of every believer: love, joy, peace, long-suffering, kindness, goodness, faithfulness, gentleness and self-control.

Growing Christians possess ALL the fruit. There is no such thing as having only the "fruit of love," or only the "fruit of gentleness." Rather, all these character traits are produced simultaneously in the life of every believer as he or she grows spiritually, because the Holy Spirit has taken residence.

If you are a growing Christian, then the fruit of the Spirit will be maturing like ripe fruit in your life.

3. God gives us GIFTS OF THE SPIRIT (1 Corinthians 12).

Gifts of the Spirit are special abilities or skills which enable each believer to contribute to the whole body (the church) of Christ with ease, pleasure and effectiveness.

For instance, if you have the gift of mercy, you do not think, "What hardship it is for me to encourage my hurting sister or brother!" Instead, you just do it. Your heart opens your home... your arms... your wallet. You wipe tears, give hugs, offer words of sympathy. And it comes naturally and with ease.

The gifts of the Spirit are given for the common good, the mutual profit of all. The Spirit's gift to you is not for your own selfish delight so you can brag about your gift. A spiritual gift always has someone else in mind, so that someone else might benefit.

God's gifts to us are good. A prayer of thanksgiving is in order. God delights in the praise of His children.

And God's giving will go on forever!

☙ GROWING RICH

1 Corinthians 12

🔥 INVESTING WISELY

Check for your spiritual gift. Ask God to help you use it effectively (see 1 Corinthians 12:8-10 for the list):

- WISDOM: applying truth to practical situations.

- KNOWLEDGE: knowing how to take steps of action based on God's Word.

- FAITH: the ability to take impossible steps for God in service.

- HEALING: the ability to minister to sick people.

- WORKING MIRACLES: the ability to move toward a faith vision and accomplish the seemingly impossible.

- PROPHECY: telling God's will from His Word.

- DISCERNING OF SPIRITS: distinguishing between the true and the false.

- TONGUES: the ability to utter ecstatic praises which build up God's name and work.

- INTERPRETATION OF TONGUES: translating the praise of God into practical application and motivation.

---

[1]Contemporary Cards @ Hallmark, Toronto, Canada. M2J 1P6 99-55.

20
Garfield Pie

onight we had Garfield pie. At least that's what Mark, our teenage son, called it. His mother, Faye, had all intentions of savouring some cherry pie left over from yesterday's dinner. But somehow the two remaining pieces deteriorated into two gaping flabs of soggy crust with only trace evidence of cherry filling smeared in between – a sad resemblance of last evening's proud dinner climax. It seems that some "mysterious Garfield" around our house had scooped out all the cherry filling, leaving the top and bottom crusts to camouflage the crime.

Faye was not impressed. Mark was served two cherry-smeared crusts – a la mode! The Great Pie Thief had received his just desserts.

Mark's pie reminded me of some people of whom Jesus spoke. Religious fakes. Counterfeit Christians who give an outward appearance of the real thing, but inside are only a mere skeleton of genuine authenticity. Right crusts outside, but only a smear of the real filling inside. Yet their deception is convincing. They sing the right songs... mouth the right platitudes... attend the right functions. The disguise is genius. But somehow it all has a hollow ring. The proper filling is missing: a generous spirit, a gracious tongue, a servant attitude. Unexpected eruptions of carnality spew acidic ashes of discord, disunity and criticism. Gently raise the lid of their inner lives, and you unleash a Pandora's swarm of resentments, caustic remarks and jealous ribbings.

Jesus had names for such phonies. Hypocrites. Blind guides. Whitewashed tombs. Snakes. Brood of vipers. He minced no words: "You look beautiful on the outside, but on the inside you are full of dead men's bones and everything unclean. On the outside, you appear as righteous, but on the inside you are full of hypocrisy and wickedness. You parade in the religious garb of legalisms and laws, but you neglect the important matters of justice, mercy and faithfulness."

Sobering thoughts indeed! We can be religious fakes.

Remedy? This is where 1 John can help. A group of phony Christians had infiltrated the Church. John refers to these teachers as antichrists (2:18), and possessing the spirit of error (4:3). The purpose of John's letter is so that we might KNOW that we live in Jesus Christ and that He in us (4:13) – so that we can be certain we are authentic. The spiritual test is two-fold:

1. An authentic believer does what is right.

"We know that we have come to Him if we obey His commands" (1 John 2:3, NIV).

It's plain and simple. We must walk as Jesus did. Obedience involves following the life-style of Jesus.

2. An authentic believer loves his brother.

"We know that we have passed from death to life, because we love our brothers.... Dear children, let us not love with words or tongue but with actions and in truth" (1 John 3:14,18, NIV).

Love is a highly desirable commodity in this age of dog-eat-dog. Practical love builds spiritual influence. Lack of love destroys our testimony.

So don't settle for soggy pie crust. Let obedience and love be your trademark. God will fill you with the delights of His rich Spirit.

🐾 GROWING RICH
Matthew 23; 1 John

🐾 INVESTING WISELY

1. *Do something to confirm your friendship this week. Send a card, write a note, take a gift.*

2. *Think of someone in a difficult circumstance. Express your love rather than judging or questioning.*

21

Disabilities Needn't Disqualify

immy had only one good arm. His other arm was a stub that ended where his elbow should have been – the result of a tragic accident.

Many children would have used such a disability as an excuse for not participating in sports. But not Jimmy. He was in my gym class. He learned how to catch a fly ball with one hand, flip the glove under his arm and whip the ball back to home plate faster than most kids with two good arms. He learned how to bat using only one arm. His skills at basketball and volleyball were evident for he made the school teams. Jimmy could even pull a football out of the air and barrel down the field for a touchdown. Jimmy did not let a disability disqualify him from his favourite sports.

Tucked away in the fine print of Old Testament genealogies is the account of a man who magnificently illustrates the truth that disabilities and handicaps need not disqualify us from success in life. His name was Jabez (see 1 Chronicles 4: 9-10).

It's difficult to imagine why a mother would name a baby Jabez. His name meant sorrow, distress or pain.

When Jabez was born, he apparently did not bring joy and happiness. His birth brought additional pain and anguish to his mother, and added to her despair.

Our imagination could run wild. Perhaps Jabez was born out of wedlock; it could be that times were tough and Jabez meant one more mouth to feed; or maybe his mother had been unfaithful and Jabez was the evidence.

Whatever the reason, Jabez grew up with the stigma of being unwanted. His name was a perpetual reminder. Talk about a disability in life! Imagine Mother introducing him to his kindergarten teacher: "His name is Pain."

But Jabez decided how to cope with this disability. He made it a matter of prayer. He asked four things of God:

1. He prayed for a superabundance of blessing.

Jabez didn't pray like so many of us: "Lord, just help me to get by and make the best of my situation. Let me be content to serve in some small corner of Your vineyard." Not Jabez! He prayed that God would make him a great winner. Triumphant. Wonderfully blessed.

2. He prayed for increased influence – an enlarged territory.

In other words, Jabez was asking God for a larger circle of ministry. I think God is pleased with that kind of praying. He wants to enlarge our circle of influence – in our staff room... across the back fence... in our children's school... on the ball team. God wants to expand our borders.

3. He prayed that God would be with him in all that he did.

Jabez knew that if God would answer "Yes" to the first two requests, he would need God's hand on all of his life. Jabez knew he would need to be sensitive to what God wanted him to say and where God wanted him to say it.

4. He prayed for God's protection – that God would keep him from harm and evil.

What was Jabez really saying to God in his prayer? He was saying, "Lord, my name is Jabez – Sorrow and Pain. I've been born under a handicap. I'm weary of it. I'm asking you to turn my life around. Stop this pattern that has been so characteristic of me. Lift this cloud from my life. Make me unique, Lord, because I have been Jabez long enough."

The chronicler records an amazing observation: God granted Jabez what he requested. As a result, he became more honourable than his brothers... more distinguished... successful... unique. Even though Jabez was the least wanted in his family, his disability did not disqualify him from success.

Two questions come to mind:

1. *What is my disability – my name, if you please?*

If I were to be named according to my disability, what might I be called? Might it be Low Self-Esteem? Poor Education? Lack of Talent? Or perhaps, I'm carrying the name of Critical. Lazy. Moody. Whatever your disability, realize that it is holding you from success.

2. *What am I doing about my disability?*

Jabez prayed, "Lord, I'm weary of being what I am, and where I am. Change my name. Take my disabilities and change them into advantages."

🍎 GROWING RICH

1 Chronicles 4:9-10; Judges 6:1-8,35; 1 Corinthians 2:1-5; 2 Corinthians 12:7-10

🍎 INVESTING WISELY

1. *You may be living under a handicap. Confess it to God. Ask Him to change your name and make a new beginning for you.*

2. *Read the biographies of great men and women who overcame their disabilities to become useful and successful: Hudson Taylor, George Muller, Fanny J. Crosby, Joni Eareckson Tada.*

— 22 —

Letter to My Son

ear Mark,

Today was a banner day!

That's because your mom and I sat in the bleachers and watched you play your best football game ever. You were the stand out leader – the star – of the Pirate's defensive squad. Not only did you play with skill and confidence, but you were the team leader on the field. You motivated, encouraged and challenged rookies and veterans alike. And when you intercepted that pass and punched over the goal line for a touchdown, I was so proud I wanted to jump up and scream like the teeny bopper girls in front of me (and also your mother!). But you know how "reserved" I am, so I just blinked back a few joy tears instead.

That touchdown proved to be the winner!

But Mark, you are not only a winner on the grid-iron, you're a winner at life too. You display a spiritual maturity that is above and beyond most teens your age. You often surpass me in your devotions and prayer life. And just as you were a leader today on your football

84

team, you are also a spiritual leader among your peers and friends. You have a unique sense of humour, and seem to squeeze every drop of enjoyment from each moment of life. May it always be so!

Thanks for being such a great guy. And keep hanging onto that ball. You've got a lot of touchdowns to score yet... on and off the football field.

Dad

Note: This letter was written to Mark after a football game he played during his last semester of high school. Mark's goal had been to someday intercept a pass and carry it into the end zone for a touchdown. That day came, and when it happened, Mark knelt on the field for a quick victory prayer, and then jumped into the air with a wild war whoop. Needless to say, it was a moving moment for his mom and dad.

GROWING RICH

2 Timothy

INVESTING WISELY

2 Timothy is a very personal and private letter written by Paul to Timothy, whom he refers to as "my dear son." Paul's reason for writing is to inspire and strengthen Timothy for his ministry in Ephesus. He reminds Timothy of his belief in him, and of the great spiritual heritage Timothy upholds from his grandmother, Lois, and his mother, Eunice. Not only that,

Paul encourages young Tim to develop the qualities in his life which characterize a Christian leader.

As you read through this letter, jot down each characteristic of a mature Christian leader. Evaluate your life in the light of these qualities. Be honest.

23
Who Cares?

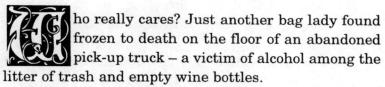ho really cares? Just another bag lady found frozen to death on the floor of an abandoned pick-up truck – a victim of alcohol among the litter of trash and empty wine bottles.

But in her youth, Drina Joubert had been a budding actress, talented poet and gifted musician. A successful modelling career had led to a screen test and offers of movie roles. She was a very beautiful woman in her younger years, but that was not evident in her later years. Twice, she was committed to a mental centre, once for threatening to kill herself. Her alcoholism worsened and she became very despondent.

A coroner's inquest attempted to piece together the 41-year-old bag lady's destructive life. Some made the comment that the system had failed. But her sister replied, "I don't know if it failed. She had a number of opportunities and I think she deliberately chose not to take them. It was her choice."

A psychiatrist who treated Drina Joubert said that she brushed aside offers of housing assistance. She suffered from alcoholism and personality disorder, but had no major illness. "She wanted to do her own thing."

Reminds me of another young man Jesus told about. He wanted to do his own thing too. He asked his dad to give him his inheritance. Off he struck for the fast lane – the big city – where he spent his time in riotous living. The boy was deceived into thinking everything would be fine. But when a severe famine arose, he began to experience a desperate situation. He was unemployed, hungry, friendless and lonely. He filled his stomach with pig feed.

But who cared? He was forgotten. Alone. Without a scrap of hope. Or so it seemed. Until he finally came to his senses.

"This is insane!" he thought. "My dad's servants eat better than this."

Suddenly, a change of heart occurred. He would go back to his dad. He carefully rehearsed his speech: "Father, I have sinned against heaven, and before you, and am no more worthy to be called your son. Make me as one of your hired servants."

His father saw him a great way off... had compassion on him... ran and fell on his neck... kissed him. The father said to his servants, "Bring the best robe, and put it on him: and put a ring on his hand, and put shoes on his feet. And bring hither the fatted calf, and kill it; and let us eat and be merry."

The father's summation was this: "My son was dead, and is alive again; he was lost and is found" (see Luke 15).

So, who cares about your life? God does. Even if you are a prodigal in a pigpen... a Drina Joubert... a gossip... a crook... a brawler... a liar... a cheat. Or even if you face nothing more than broken promises, silent rooms and barren walls. God cares. Reach out to Him. A flame will rekindle in your heart. As Fanny Crosby sang:

> *Down in human heart,*
> *Crushed by the tempter,*
> *Feelings lie buried that grace can restore.*
> *Touched by a loving heart,*
> *Wakened by kindness,*
> *Chords that were broken will vibrate once more.*

Only God can build trophies from the scrap pile. The adulteress, dope addict, hypocrite, playboy, misfit or drop out. You name it – His grace is sufficient.

And talk about a homecoming! Yellow ribbons 'round the old oak tree! When we come to the Heavenly Father,

- the angels of Heaven rejoice.
- He writes our name in the Book of Life.
- He re-designates our status to "Saint."
- And we get in on the greatest feast ever prepared: the Marriage Supper of Jesus Christ and His Church.

The choice is ours: turn aside from God's offer of forgiveness and help; or respond to a new life in Christ Jesus.

Up from the trash pile! Home to Father!

GROWING RICH

Luke 15; Isaiah 61

🦥 INVESTING WISELY

Eternal life with the Heavenly Father is yours by simply praying the suggested prayer:

"Lord Jesus, I invite you into my life as Saviour and Lord. Forgive my sins: rebellion, carelessness, stubbornness, dishonesty. Make me the kind of person you want me to be. I will live for you from this moment on."

If this prayer expresses the desires of your heart, Christ will come into your life as He promised. Read 1 John 5:11-13 for assurance.

24
Helena's Song

elena seldom speaks to anyone. Her face is blank. She only blinks and stares into space. There is no recognition. No response.

Helena has Alzheimer's. She doesn't seem to know that I am standing at her bedside, which has been pushed temporarily into the busy hallway of our local hospital. She hasn't spoken to me in months. Nothing I do gets her attention.

Her sister sits at the foot of the bed, massaging Helena's toes. "Try singing 'Jesus Loves Me,' or 'What A Friend We Have In Jesus,'" her sister urges. "Helena responds to them."

Now, I'm not much for singing in a busy hospital hall next door to the nursing station. But this time, pride takes a back seat and I lean down and look directly into Helena's far away eyes. Ignoring the bustling activity of hospital hall mania, I clear my throat and begin to sing: "Jesus loves me, this I know..."

Hardly do I begin when Helena's gaze turns to mine. Her eyes focus and a chord of recognition sweeps aside the cobwebs of her foggy memory. With halting voice, but in perfect key, she joins to sing:

91

> *Jesus loves me, this I know,*
> *For the Bible tells me so.*
> *Little ones to Him belong,*
> *They are weak, but He is strong.*

Without pause, and oblivious to the smiles of passing hospital personnel and the upturned heads at the nursing station, we continue our hymn sing:

> *What a friend we have in Jesus,*
> *All our sins and griefs to bear.*
> *What a privilege to carry,*
> *Everything to God in prayer.*

For one brief moment, Helena and I were reunited in spirit. Pastor and patient – one in the Lord. Somewhere in Helena's subconscious is filed the comforting truth that Jesus loves her, and cares.

The singing soon ends and the misty haze returns. Comprehension vanishes and the focus is gone. I bow to pray. But Helena only stares and blinks.

As I turn to leave, my ear is tuned to music in the distant yonder. Seems to me I hear the strains of heavenly singing. Two voices are blending together in perfect unison. They are standing before the glorious throne of God. Helena has looked me up. We are singing a new song:

> *Blessings and glory and thanksgiving,*
> *To our God who sits upon the throne.*

And God replies, "See, I am making all things new." Former pastor. Former patient. Perfect understanding!

🎵 GROWING RICH

Revelation 7:9-17; 22

🎵 INVESTING WISELY

Stop in to visit a lonely shut-in. Take along a snack. Read an encouraging portion of the Bible to them. And take your hymn book – and sing!

25
Humble Image

here I was peeking through the bars. Yes, the senior pastor of Centennial Road Standard Church was in jail. Locked in the slammer. Crime? Sporting a "Humble Image"!

The court summons arrived in the mail:

> To Laurence Croswell.
>
> WHEREAS you have been charged with a
>   "Humble Image."
> THEREFORE, this is to command you to
>   attend before the presiding judge or justice
> on the 28th day of April,
>   at 1:10 p.m.,
>   at the 1000 Island Mall.

Humble image? Seems a certain joker tipped off a police officer that I had been seen driving a rusty clunker. Our second car was thirteen years old and suffering the ravages of the cankerous salt applied to icy streets. My boys called it the Green Tank.

"Your Honour," roared the crown prosecutor at the Mall Court. "Pastor Croswell is playing 'humble.' Sets a poor image in our city. Chooses to make pastoral calls in an old rust bucket, even though he owns a better car. He mocks the word, 'humility,' because he's playing poor. Why, he has even been mistaken for a transient. This is not appropriate for a man of the cloth.

"I recommend, Your Honour, that he be sentenced to prison and fined $150."

"What is your defense, Reverend?" The judge peered at me and waited for an answer. I mumbled something about hard times for pastors and too much salt on winter roads.

"Guilty as charged!" declared the judge, and slammed his gavel to finalize his decision.

A uniformed officer led me to the Mall Jail and locked the door until such time as the fine should be paid.

Relax! My court appearance was only a publicity stunt to help raise funds for the local Crime Stoppers. My stay in the cardboard jail was only in fun. I was shortly released from my makeshift prison cell, and the fine for my crime was paid in full.

But there is a lesson to be learned from my court debut, because Jesus had a lot to say about those who sport a false façade. Jesus called them hypocrites. False prophets. Ravenous wolves. Whitewashed tombs. Outside, they appear beautiful and clean; but inside, they are full of dead man's bones and all uncleanness. Note the quality of their life from Matthew 7:

- they are fault finders (vs. 1-6);
- their prayer life is weak (vs. 7-11);
- they have a hidden agenda (vs. 15-20);
- their words are a lie (vs. 21-23).

So, if you can't hide from the long arm of the Crime Stoppers Crew, how can you hide from an all-seeing God? Someday the Eternal Judge will declare the hidden truth of our lives. There will be a lot of excuses and explanations... but they won't stand up in the Court of Heaven.

So off with our masks. Be honest before God. Admit our sins. Count on Him to forgive and thoroughly cleanse us from all that is evil (see 1 John 1:9). We'll have nothing to hide, and no record will be kept against us.

By the way, I drove the old clunker to the junk heap the other day. Left behind a multitude of mechanical headaches and deteriorating fender walls.

No more sporting a humble image for me. And no more raised eyebrows from my police friend.

What a relief!

👥 GROWING RICH

Matthew 7:13-27; Matthew 23:27-39

👥 INVESTING WISELY

Look at yourself in a mirror. Ask God to reveal the "real you." Is there a spirit of arrogance? Pride? Fault finding? Self-righteousness? Confess your "mask" to God. You'll breathe a sigh of relief in His forgiveness and cleansing.

26

Laugh Again, Live A Lot

The most natural thing in the world for an eleven-year-old boy is laughter. A few nights ago when I came in for dinner, I noted a string of spaghetti clutching the wall above the baker's cupboard.

"How did spaghetti fly up there?" I asked. My family was already seated around the dinner table.

Darren snickered. "Like this, Dad." He pulled a long piece of spaghetti from his plate, twirled it around and around... and let it fly.

Swish, Swish, Swish! It rotated through the air like a pasta helicopter until it plopped on the kitchen ceiling above our heads. It hung there, neatly nestled like a snake on a rock. Howls of laughter erupted from around the kitchen table. Even the mother of this raucous crew wiped tears of laughter from her face.

It was a happy moment. Harmless joke. Feast of spaghetti. Joy and laughter.

But why is happiness an elusive dream for many? Why are moments so few when families and friends experience simple joy together? Instead of laughter, why the old worn record of IF ONLY? I'd be happy...

- IF ONLY it were the weekend.
- IF ONLY I had a different job.
- IF ONLY I had a bigger house.
- IF ONLY my husband would give up golf.

Jesus wanted his followers to experience joy without IF ONLYS. In fact, He considered it so important that He called His disciples aside from busy ministry and shared eight simple formulas... eight "Be Happy Attitudes" guaranteed to bring inner joy in the hectic days ahead. They seemed for all the world to contradict the spirit of happiness, but Jesus guaranteed their "blessedness":

1. Oh, the joy of honestly admitting my weakness! The poor in spirit get into God's family.

2. Oh, the joy of being desperate enough to change! When I mourn over sin, I receive God's forgiveness.

3. Oh, the joy of staying calm, cool and collected when the world is upside-down! The meek are promoted and trusted.

4. Oh, the joy of wanting these attitudes so badly that I think I'll die without them! The hungry and thirsty will be filled.

5. Oh, the joy of realizing my own shortcomings! I am sympathetic towards others. God will give me mercy and so will others.

6. Oh, the joy of revealing my feelings! My heart is pure and nothing blocks my view of God.

7. Oh, the joy of being under God's control! I am qualified to bring harmony to home, school and church.

8. Rejoice! Some will be upset with my lifestyle. But it doesn't matter because Jesus said I am in great company.

Jesus made things simple, not complicated. Even a kindergarten student could understand the application of these attitudes to life:

1. Be kind to others.
2. Be honest.
3. Be moral.
4. Marry for life.
5. Go the second mile.
6. Do good to your enemies.

Simple living! Easily understood, easily followed. No jamming the brain with computer overload. You'll have time to smell the roses and relax. Unwind. You may even see humour in flying spaghetti! You'll laugh again, and live a lot.

🐾 GROWING RICH

Matthew 5

🐾 INVESTING WISELY

Memorize the Beatitudes (Be Happy Attitudes from Matthew 5:3-12). Recite them before you close your eyes in sleep, and when you awaken during the night.

27
The Great Zucchini

 e billed himself "The Great Zucchini." It was one of those crazy adult church socials where everyone lets down his hair and laughs till his sides ache. Alec was the featured entertainer and he was doing a take-off on the illusive illusionist, Houdini. He dashed to the stage appropriately costumed in flowing cape and green velvet turban.

And now... "LAADIEEES and GENNNTLEMEN!" he announced with gusto. "I will hammer a watch into smithereens. And right before your very eyes, I will mysteriously put it back together again. But I need a volunteer. Will someone please volunteer their watch?"

No one budged.

"Pastor! Will you lend your watch to me? It's for a good cause." Zucchini looked straight at me. I squirmed, but agreed. I handed over my silver Timex.

Carefully, Zucchini spread a large handkerchief over the watch and picked up the hammer. He brandished the hammer over his head like a war tomahawk, and with pompous vigor, proceeded to pound the watch to break it into little pieces. He then muttered some hocus pocus incantation and swooped the handkerchief away.

Would the watch be intact? No such luck! There laid a twisted conglomeration of springs, broken crystal and bent hands. How would Zucchini explain his apparent failure? "Oh well, you win some and lose some." He nonchalantly tossed the twisted pieces into the garbage can.

Peals of laughter erupted from the audience. I wiped tears from my eyes – not because I was grieving my loss, but because Alec had swapped watches previous to his performance and some in the audience were certain he had mortally wounded Pastor's watch. Zucchini's performance was a big fake! The performance was hilarious.

We smile when the Great Zucchini fails. That's expected of him. But it is shameful when a Christian fails to perform the works of Jesus Christ and claims authenticity.

That embarrassment happened one day to some perplexed disciples. They found themselves powerless to help a desperate father and his ill son. When Jesus appeared on the scene, the father brushed aside the disciples and rushed to Jesus. "Lord," he begged, "have mercy on my son."

With one strong word of rebuke, Jesus took the lad and lifted him to his feet. Cured.

There is something modern about this story. Why is it that we, the modern disciples of Jesus, are so powerless to meet the crying need of human suffering? Loneliness. Overstress. Anxiety. Fatigue. Disillusionment. Brokenness. Like Zucchini, we can only shrug, shake our heads and admit failure. If only we could be like Jesus – react to crisis with composure... move with confidence... provide answers to life's pressing problems.

What is the solution to our dilemma? Jesus provided the answer. Spiritual power comes by spending time alone with God and His Word – the daily discipline of the secret place (Mark 9:29). So simple. Yet, so fundamental.

Jesus practised what He preached. Mark tells us that in the morning, Jesus rose up a great while before daybreak, went into a solitary place and there prayed. Jesus was authentic. That's why He had power.

A fake will never be great. Authentic people draw strength from God and give it to others.

🐾 GROWING RICH

Matthew 17:14-20

🐾 INVESTING WISELY

Dear Heavenly Father,

I open my inner life to You. Cleanse me from sinful thoughts and motives. Increase my faith and fill me with Your power. Lead me to someone in need. May I be Your ministering servant. Amen.

28
Good News From the Olden Days

 ad, what was it like to live in the olden days – when you were young?"

The question jolted me. Don't my sons realize that I am not a fossil... some ancient artifact excavated from an anthropological dig, about to be catalogued and stored away for posterity? After all, I'm only middle-aged! Full of vim and vigour! Up-to-date!

Still... the question stopped me in my tracks. Sights and sounds that were once familiar to me and events that occurred daily in my boyhood on the farm are foreign to my two sons.

They have not experienced the joy of milking by hand a newly freshened cow, and training her calf to drink from a pail.

They have never spent the day wrestling the steering wheel of a stubborn, two-cylinder John Deere tractor, slowly plodding across forty acres of summerfallow.

They have never, on a cold wintry day, tasted home-made soup simmered atop a wood-coal stove in a one-room country school.

They have never passed a summer's day pitching stoneboat loads of rotted cow manure across an acre garden plot, and then hoeing the pesky pig weed that also loved the fertilizing.

Yes, life is different now than when I was ten. Perhaps more than I care to admit to those smart-aleck boys. They have never experienced the "olden days" on a mixed farm in northern Alberta. They do not understand the sights, sounds and smells that were so familiar to me while I was growing up.

UNFAMILIAR SHEPHERD SCENE

Such is the case with the shepherd scene in John 10. The scene was most familiar in first century Palestine. To us it is foreign and unfamiliar. We have never seen a shepherd, raw-boned and leathery-skinned, let alone understand the vocabulary of his trade. But the vocabulary and imagery were known to almost everyone who heard Jesus. The shepherd and sheep on the hillside were as familiar to Jesus as the milk pail and cream-separator were to the barefoot boy in the old farm barnyard of yesteryear.

Sheep knew the voice of their shepherd. The shepherd had the ability to talk to his sheep in a sing-song voice, sometimes clucking in his throat. The sheep knew and understood the eastern shepherd's voice and would come leaping toward him. At times, the shepherd would call sharply to remind the sheep that he was still there... but if the stranger should call, they would flee.

Flocks were often collected into open-air sheepfolds – a simple wall enclosure. There was no door, but at night, the shepherd would lie across the opening. He literally became "the door" and no sheep could stray, nor could a wolf enter.

JESUS, THE GOOD SHEPHERD

Every detail of the Palestinian shepherd lights up the picture of Jesus, the Good Shepherd. His sheep hear His voice, and He constantly cares for His flock. He is the door to abundant life now, and eternal life to come. The Good Shepherd voluntarily laid Himself down and gave His life for His sheep – you and me. No thief nor robber can snatch us out of His hand.

My boys have never lived on a farm in the "olden days," but when they listen to their dad reminisce, they can learn valuable lessons about life.

I have never been a shepherd in the time of Jesus, but when I read that Jesus is my Good Shepherd, I learn lessons about his deep love and care for me.

That's good news from the olden days that I can understand today!

🐾 GROWING RICH

John 10:1-30

🐾 INVESTING WISELY

Reserve a quiet block of time. Open your Bible to John 10. Read. Meditate. Listen. Hear the inner voice of the Good Shepherd. He is calling. Directing. Leading. Follow the Good Shepherd and align yourself with His purpose for your life.

29

Tanya From Chernobyl

esterday, Faye was at the Farmer's Market and met Ed Bell, one of the teachers from our local public school. Ed was emotional. He and his wife, Joanne, had just said good-bye to a little Russian girl who had been with them for the past six weeks. Tanya was a victim of the terrible Chernobyl disaster that spilled radio-active material across the luscious pastures of her homeland.

When Tanya got off the bus in Brockville, she was as grey as cement. Her teeth were black with decay, her hair chopped off and her body frail and thin. She carried a little red backpack with all her belongings in it: two flimsy skirts, a pair of threadbare underwear and some thin socks that looked like boys' socks. She wore a pair of hole-ridden track pants and a flimsy sweater.

"That's it!" exclaimed Joanne, later recounting the story to me. "That's all she brought to spend six weeks in Canada! She looked like a little frightened kitten."

For six weeks, Tanya lived with the Bells and their daughter. She shared their home, food, clothing and money. Tanya got her teeth fixed – twenty-two fillings, four extractions and two root-canals (when she came home from the dentist she ate two hot dogs – no problem!).

Tanya was fitted with glasses and given a medical check-up. She frolicked on the roller coasters at Canada's Wonderland. The Bells gave this little Russian girl the best time she ever had.

On Friday, they sent her back home with one hundred pounds of baggage – new clothes, medication, toiletries and two bottles of ketchup.

Joanne said that when Tanya got on the plane, she was brown and plump like a bunny. Her teeth were white, her skin healthy and she could see through new glasses. When they said good-bye, they all cried like babies. But there was a warm feeling inside because they had taken the opportunity to show compassion and it felt good.

SUFFERING – AN OPPORTUNITY

Suffering is everywhere. How do we respond to a hurting world? Jesus shows us that suffering is an opportunity for God's people to show compassion... to let the Light of the World shine through our lives in practical ways.

In John 9, Jesus becomes involved with a man born blind. He had never seen his mother's face... never seen a twinkling star... never seen the unfolding beauty of a wild flower. What does Jesus do? He stops and becomes involved. He spits on the ground, mixes it to form clay (saliva in the ancient world was often used as medicine) and puts it on the man's eyes. Jesus uses the customs of the day to build this man's faith. "Now," he says, "Go and wash in the Pool of Siloam."

The man taps his way through the narrow streets until he comes to kneel on his hands and knees beside the pool. Then he begins to wash his eyes. Suddenly, he starts to see his own reflection in the rippling pool of water. For the first time in his life, he sees his face and his hands. He raises his eyes to see a panorama of sights around him. He shouts for joy and dances in excitement. He raises his hands to worship. He makes his way back to Jesus and, for the first time, he looks at people.

When the neighbours hear about the blind man's healing, they respond with skepticism. No one is elated. No one is joyful that the blind can see. They gather about in huddles and doubt.

The Pharisees condemn the whole affair. They are exasperated. After all, hadn't Jesus healed on the Sabbath, and isn't that against regulations?

But watch the little blind man. He's grinning from ear to ear... even though he's been excommunicated. All he knows is that once he was blind and now he can see. And Jesus did it! I think he does another little hop-skip-and-jump, and gives God the glory.

Suffering is an opportunity to display what God can do. We may not tell people to pick up their beds and walk, or anoint their eyes with clay and give them sight. But we can pray and supply a lame man with crutches, or provide a little girl from Russia with glasses. Christians have become involved with these kinds of activities for ages. They have been pace-setters in providing practical service to help a suffering world. It's what Jesus would do.

The blessings and benefits can't be measured in dollars and cents. For those involved, there is inner joy that can't be described or explained.

If you don't believe me, just ask the Bells.

Better still, try reaching out to someone in need yourself.

🐟 GROWING RICH

John 9

🐟 INVESTING WISELY

Do you know a disabled person? Think of a practical way to supply a need or provide a service. Volunteer to give a care-giver a much needed break.

30

Making Champions

orgive me, I can't resist a little braggadocio. I have two sons who learned what it means to be champions – in different ways, but winners nevertheless.

Mark, the older, plays defensive end for his high-school football team and last night, his picture was in the newspaper. The caption read: "TISS Pirates 'Mark Croswell' (17) goes up to break the pass intended for BCI Red Rams in action at TISS on Friday."

Now understand, the picture is only the icing. It's what it took to get there that makes me proud. Three years ago, Mark announced that he was going to play football. That's right, little skinny Mark – the son I could Indian wrestle to the ground with ease – wanted to face those humongous bruisers on the gridiron.

I was skeptical, but Mark was determined. Every-day, he pumped weights. That summer, he went to training camp. He learned to stalk a wide receiver, run interference and make crushing tackles. He nursed torn ligaments, sprained ankles and black bruises. Seldom did he complain or miss a practice.

Mark has since been named to two All-Star Teams,

and his dad no longer challenges him to Indian wrestling! Best of all, he has maintained a strong witness to his Christian faith.

Then there is Darren, the younger son. The other night, he played Tom Sawyer – the lead roll in his school musical. It was a major production with costumes, lights and choreography. Many hours had gone into making it a classy presentation.

But on opening day, Darren came down with the flu. He had it all. Fever, headache, achy bones and upset stomach. Would weeks of memorizing lines and rehearsing songs be for naught? Darren gritted his teeth, swallowed tylenol and performed on pure adrenalin. He made his pale bow to the standing ovation of the audience. His dad clapped the loudest.

Champions rise to the occasion. That's why I was proud of Mark and Darren. Champions are not more talented or gifted than others. They just have more grit, determination and faith.

That's what makes the Hall of Faith Champions in Hebrews 11 so attractive. What a variety of personalities the writer lists for our spiritual motivation! Some were frightened, others were helpless; some were destitute, and many more were unknown. But they all gritted their teeth, dug in their heels and persevered by faith. Despite hardships and handicaps, they were faith winners who subdued kingdoms, shut the mouths of lions and instituted change.

The important thing is that all of them persisted. They continued to believe the impossible despite overwhelming odds. That's why Hebrews 12 continues by saying, "Look around at the winners! Stay in the running!

Look at Jesus Christ! He was the originator and finisher of our faith. Our Lord endured far more than any other hero. He endured the cross. As we look to Him, He increases our faith and gives us the strength to rise up and win."

You're surrounded by a grandstand of cheerleaders. While others are frightened, you can be confident.

Don't faint. Endure and win.

🐾 GROWING RICH

Hebrews 11-12:3

🐾 INVESTING WISELY

Write out what your philosophy in life will be and what it will take for you to be successful in life. Ask yourself:

1. *Do I welcome challenges with optimism?*

2. *Do I convey confidence?*

3. *Do I quit easily, or do I get up and keep going?*

4. *Do I restrict thinking to established patterns, or am I creative and highly fluid?*

5. *Do I exhibit a pattern of faith in my life decisions?*

31
King Fluff

here's this humming bird who has taken own-
ership of my artificial feeder. He's the epito-
me of greed, pure and simple! He sits aloft on
an oak branch overlooking the sugar water and thinks
he's king of the castle. The little guy is on a power trip,
and dive bombs all intruding hummers – "a glowing
ember with the hum of a fighter jet." He won't share. He
perches on his twig throne arrogantly fluffing his incan-
descent feathers – one nickel's weight of feather power
glistening in the sun.

Sad thing is, there are four feeding straws – quite
enough for friends to sit and share a drink. They could
take turns, and I would fill the jar when it got empty.
The supply is endless. No one need go hungry.

But not with King Fluff around. He's decided he
owns the feeder. My back yard is his territory to control,
manage and protect.

Tragedy happened this morning. A young female
whirred off in hasty retreat and smacked into the picture window. Died on the spot. Massive concussion.
And while I removed the unfortunate victim, King
Fluff buzzed past my head to frighten off another

would-be feeder. Seems he'll never learn. Greed works that way.

King Fluff reminds me of people governed by greed. They've forgotten that God is Creator and all things come from Him. Instead, they stake out their territory, puff out their chests and crown themselves little kings. They want power, money and domination at any cost. No price is too high. They'll even dive bomb the weak and helpless.

Too bad! There is enough for all, if everyone shared. Gave a little. Took a cut.

Sad thing is, so many innocents get caught in the greedy cross-fire – children, widows, elderly. Their cries are everywhere – in crowded apartments, foodbanks and back alleys; in ghettos, refugee camps and war-torn cities.

A RICH MAN, POOR OVERNIGHT

Jesus told of a greedy man. He decided to tear down his barns and build bigger barns. There was no word of sharing. No ministry mind-set. He just wanted to have more.

"Fool!" said Jesus. "This night your soul will be required." The rich man became poor overnight.

Pity! The man could have helped so many. Instead? Greedy heirs probably squandered his fortune away.

🐌 GROWING RICH

Luke 12:16-21; 21:1-4

INVESTING WISELY

Give something away today. A freshly-baked cake. One hour's worth of help. A cup of coffee and a listening ear. A ride. Check your will. Does it include God's work?

—— 32 ——

Run to Win

"Did you win, Mommy? Did you win?" Four-year-old Katherine hopped about excitedly, splashing cool water into the sweat-soaked face of her exhausted mother.

"When I grow up, I want to wear a number and run a race too!" Katherine announced. "Just like you, Mommy!" Anita wobbled on rubbery legs between the supporting arms of husband Rick, and big brother Dan.

Who cared if Mommy had barely dragged across the finish line of the 10 kilometer run – just ahead of the clean-up crew and the red flashing light of the Police cruiser? Not Katherine. Her mommy had run in the big race. And finished!

Certainly her mommy had won. After all, she had crossed the finish line, hadn't she? Winners always cross the finish line.

THE FAITH RACE

The apostle Paul was always fascinated by the picture of the runner. He knew that an athlete runs to win. For some, it's placing first in the field; for others (like

116

Anita), it's just crossing the finish line. Paul draws upon the familiar scene of the runner when he writes to share practical spiritual insights with young believers in the faith.

1. TO WIN: DECIDE TO BEGIN (Hebrews 12:1).

One thing is certain. The person who does not start can never win.

Take courage from the great cloud of spiritual champions who have begun and won before us. They are overcomers. Tough times didn't stop them. Discouragement didn't turn them. Threats of death didn't deter them (see Hebrews 11).

2. TO ENDURE: DETERMINE TO DISCIPLINE (1 Corinthians 9:24-27).

A serious athlete disciplines to win. He is temperate in all things; brings his body into subjection; develops a positive winning attitude.

Finishing the faith race requires discipline. It begins with a daily quiet time with God and His Word. But it also includes weeding out negative thoughts, rejecting discouragement and deciding to do whatever is necessary to finish the task at hand.

Remember. To be undisciplined in our faith race is to have one foot in the sand and the other on a banana peel!

3. TO FINISH: DIRECT YOUR EYES TO THE PRIZE (Philippians 3:14).

Don't be a drop out. Reach forward to those things which are ahead. Plan and chart your course. Forget those things which are behind. Set goals. Rise to higher plateaus. BE A WINNER.

So develop the winner's edge. Give your all. Go for it! Crossing the finish line is exhilarating! Just ask Anita.

GROWING RICH

Hebrews 11; 12:1-15; 1 Corinthians 9:24-27; Philippians 3:12-21

INVESTING WISELY

"Dear God, thank you for this boost You have given me. Today I shall begin to move closer toward the goal You have set for my life. I will give 100 percent effort. I know there is a divine purpose behind my life. Thank you, God, for enabling me to make this exciting discovery. Amen."

33

When God Says No

ometimes God says NO. A young woman had trained and been appointed for missionary service. With great anticipation, she looked forward to serving God on a foreign field. But tragedy struck. Her sister died leaving four small children behind. There seemed no other choice but to stay home and care for the motherless family. Her heart was broken. She could not understand why God would say NO to her dream of serving as a missionary. However, she submitted to His will and began to invest her life in the four little children.

Time passed. Each child grew and graduated from high school. One by one, they came to their faithful aunt, saying, "Auntie, I feel that God wants me to be a missionary." God had said NO the first time, only to multiply the dream four-fold.

Perhaps you have experienced a slammed door on your dreams:

- Marks that did not quite reach entrance qualifications;

- A promotion that fluttered out of reach;

- An accident that permanently disabled;
- Ministry expectations that suddenly evaporated.

Your dream has been noble. But God says, "This is not for your life." Your plans are stopped cold. Snuffed out. Why?

Fortunately, God has recorded examples in His Word for insight and instruction. The "Broken Dream Syndrome" is beautifully addressed in the life of David. In 2 Samuel 7, David is at rest in his magnificent new palace. He is surrounded by luxury – intricate stone masonry, lavish carpets and draperies, carved furnishings. David has every reason to relax and to be content with his prosperity. But one factor troubles his conscience and keeps him from enjoying his good fortune to the fullest. He has not prepared a place of comparable splendor for the sacred symbol of God's presence, the Ark.

"Do you see how I dwell in a house of cedar, but the Ark of God dwells in a tent of curtain?" David asks the trusted prophet, Nathan.

"Go do all that is in your heart, for the Lord is with you," Nathan encourages him.

A great joy surges through David, for the prophet's words seem to indicate a green light. David could now set about building a magnificent house for God. He could demonstrate his gratitude for God's blessing.

But David's dream is squelched the very next morning. Nathan returns with this announcement: "Thus says the Lord... your son after you shall build a house for My Name."

Talk about a firm NO! Talk about the death of a vision! It won't be David. It will be his son.

How do you handle disappointments? What is my response to slammed doors and firm NOs?

Here is what David does:

1. **HE PRAYS and seeks God's redirection** (2 Sam. 7:18-21). No hint of resentment. Just gratitude and trust.

2. **HE PRAISES and worships God** (2 Sam. 7:22-26). Out of a sense of awe, David expresses wonder and amazement for the ways of God.

3. **HE PLANS an unselfish response.** David enthusiastically makes arrangements to gather all the building materials for the construction of a temple he will never see. Someone else will get the glory. His own testimony reads, "I have prepared with all my might for the house of my God" (1 Chron. 29:2). May his tribe increase!

Remember, God's perspective is not my perspective. God's picture is not my picture. God's plan is always from an eternal viewpoint. His NO often means YES to something bigger and better than I could ever imagine or think.

🙢 GROWING RICH

2 Samuel 7; 1 Chronicles 28, 29

🙢 INVESTING WISELY

Consider these exhortations when God says NO:

1. RE-EVALUATE. *Be flexible. Be open to change. Don't give in to bitterness and blame. Ask God to give you wisdom to know how to respond.*

2. RE-DIRECT *your efforts to help someone else fulfill your dream. Your role may be different than you ever expected.*

3. RESURRECTION *will come from God. Trust Him. Someday you will see the big picture. The pieces will fit together. It's God's perfect plan.*

34
Louisa's Gift

 ouisa's gift makes me wince! I was teaching Grade 4, and Louisa, a little Greek girl, was in my class. Louisa was special. For a short while, she had been a foster child in the home of my parents-in-law at their farm near Forester's Falls. When she reunited with her mother, Louisa moved back to Brockville and was delighted to be placed in my classroom at Prince of Wales School where I taught. I was her security blanket in a class of strange faces, and I treated her as my special friend.

One evening, Faye and I were invited to Louisa's home for dinner. Louisa was there, beaming, translating for her Greek-speaking mother and scurrying about to help set the table. The meal was entirely home cooked. Authentic Greek food. Hot, steaming and delicious. One of the dishes was like small cabbage rolls, only wrapped with grape leaves. "Mmmm!" I gushed as I plopped the petite rolls into my mouth. "They're delicious!" Louisa smiled with delight. She was pleased that her teacher was her friend and was enjoying the dinner she and her mom had worked so long to prepare.

After a few days, I was preparing for class during the break after lunch when I noticed a brown bag on my desk with no name on it. It was moist and slightly dripping, and I assumed that one of the children had carelessly left their lunch remains behind – on my desk! But the bag was still bulging, so I gingerly opened it for a peek to see whether the contents were worthwhile returning to an owner (I don't like wasting food), or whether I should just garbage the remains.

Peering inside, I turned up my nose in disgust. An unusual aroma greeted me that I took for being slightly stale. The contents, wrapped in wax paper, were wet, and turning green.

"Yuk!" I thought. "Someone has found this old lunch bag with spoiling food and put it on my desk. Some trick!"

I gingerly dropped the bag into the wastebasket and thought no more about it until the bell rang to call my students back to class. That's when Louisa came bursting excitedly into the room. She came to my desk looking for a bag she had placed there. And when she didn't see it, she looked beside my desk and spotted it – in the wastebasket! She pulled it out with horror. There was hurt in her eyes and her voice as she said, "Mr. Croswell! This is your present! A special treat! Greek food... wrapped in grape leaves!"

A sick feeling shuddered in the pit of my stomach. I had taken Louisa's gift and treated it with contempt. An irreverent act of disrespect. It was unintentional, but I had thrown away the gift Louisa and her mom had carefully prepared and wrapped for me. Louisa had brought the gift because she liked me a lot, but I had thrown it into the garbage can.

Now, while you are working through the strong emotion of the scene in my classroom, you can understand how God must feel about His children. He has given us gifts – special motivations and skills to carry out His work. They have been carefully prepared and packaged to fit into our lives so that we might find meaning in carrying out an important function in His Body, the Church. God wants us to use them. If we do, we'll be surprised at how successful we will become. They will give us meaning and fulfillment.

But sadly, many of God's children have simply discarded these gifts... turned up their noses and carelessly thrown them aside – into some excuse basket. They've never used them. They've scorned them. They've never found the fulfillment of being involved.

I open my Bible to James 1 and place my finger under verse 17. Here is what it says to me about God's gifts: "Every good gift and every perfect gift is from above, and comes down from the Father of lights...."

Notice: Every good and perfect gift comes from God. Now, don't misunderstand. This is not some random gift tossed out carelessly and indiscriminately. This gift has YOU in mind... not to collect dust or be discarded, but to be used in a unique capacity for God.

"Stir up the gift of God within you" (2 Tim. 1:6). Get involved. Prayerfully determine your motivating spiritual gift from Romans 12:6-8. Develop the weaker ones too.

1. **PROPHECY:** Telling God's truth and the results that come from following or disobeying.

2. **SERVING:** Meeting practical needs to help others.

3. **TEACHING:** Telling what God's Word means and how it applies to our lives.

4. **EXHORTING:** Encouraging others to live Christ-filled lives and giving them practical steps to follow.

5. **GIVING:** Sharing money and goods to help ministries flourish.

6. **MERCY:** Practical involvement to help heal people's hurts.

GROWING RICH

Romans 12:6-8; 1 Corinthians 12

INVESTING WISELY

Dear Heavenly Father,

Thank you for placing precious gifts in my life. I know your Spirit will empower me to use these gifts to serve You. I will use each gift with grace and love, as I interact with others. I offer you my hands, my feet, my voice and my mind. Amen.

35

Dawna's Diary

A lot can happen in just one week – especially in December near Christmas time. Just ask Dawna, my sister-in-law. She telephoned Faye the other night with true confessions to fill an entire Murphy's Law Calendar for the coming year. Listen in on her conversation. You might identify with her week:

"Last week was horrendous. It began on the weekend. The office where I work is computerizing. We discovered a mistake that went back five years in our records. Guess what? I spent the entire weekend tracing the errors. Yes... Saturday evening and Sunday evening until 11 p.m.

"In the meantime, Allan (husband) returned from his doctor's appointment. He was down; his cholesterol was up. More dieting.

"Then Olivia (daughter) became ill. She slept for twenty-seven hours straight, got up for a short while and then slept for another thirty-one. I rushed her to the doctor. As we left his office, Olivia passed out in the busy hall of the health clinic. Medical people rushed to assist; multitudes surrounded to watch. 'It's a virus,' the doctor said.

"Back at the homefront, Jonathan (son) was desperately working to complete a school project. He couldn't do it without my assistance. We frantically worked to meet the deadline (which he knew about for a number of weeks in advance!).

"Oh yes, Nugget (dog) threw up on the living room carpet. Too many Christmas treats.

"Yesterday, Jonathan returned from a trip to the basement. 'Mom, there's water in YOUR basement!' It couldn't be! No flooding now! Sure enough, my exquisitely wrapped Christmas gifts – the ones I had purchased special paper and expensive bows for – lay in pools of water. We had forgotten to drain the line when we stored the garden hose. I am in process of restocking Christmas ribbons and paper.

"Tonight, I couldn't even zap us a quick supper. My microwave died.

"Yes, we are looking forward to a quiet Christmas because now I have bronchitis."

A blizzard of troubles. I thought of changing the names to protect the afflicted, but I wanted you to know that this story is true. And it's not atypical. Happens in hundreds of households. Probably yours. Christians aren't exempt. Simply change a few circumstances and names, and you could be the main character in the plot.

Friends ask, "How are you doing?" You give the pat answer: "Oh, fine! Just great! Fantastic!" But you know it's not true. Inside, you know the bank account won't balance, your children are irritable and cranky, and you're overstressed and overworked.

Irritations. Complications. Temptations. How do we cope? Get by? Come out on top? What does the Bible have to say about life where you live? I mean, real life with headaches and heartbreaks?

Listen to the apostle Paul:

"We are troubled on every side, yet not distressed; we are perplexed but not in despair; persecuted, but not forsaken; cast down, but not destroyed" (2 Cor. 4:8,9).

The Bible is a practical book, but is not a magic repellent to rub on yourself twice daily to keep the devil away... not a miracle pill to swallow for overnight growth... not a list of fool-proof formulas to produce instant success. The Bible is a road map. A survivor's guide. A light to guide us through the dark valleys. Tough times won't last forever, and greener meadows are on the other side. But first, faith is increased. God proves Himself faithful. Character growth will be the outcome.

When irritations strike, trust God. When complications arise, set time aside to hear God's voice. When temptations lure, recite truths of Scripture. When sin invades, apply the principles you have been taught. This is more than just grin-and-bear-it theology. This is taking the Bible seriously and allowing the words to pervade your inner life. The Holy Spirit will provide the power to see you through. James indicates that we will be perfect and entire, wanting nothing (James 1:4).

So don't dodge problems. Attack them with God's Word. Handle them with prayer. Gear up and confront... stop running away. Conquer set backs. God will build beauty from ashes and do a work that will surprise you.

Tomorrow, by God's grace, we will emerge stronger and wiser on the other side. We will persevere through the pressure. But never alone. We are not forsaken, not struck down, not perplexed. The Lord Jesus is with us every step of the way.

Ready for next week, Dawna?

🔖 GROWING RICH

2 Corinthians 4:7-18

🔖 INVESTING WISELY

Set aside next Sunday as a day of rest. Worship at church. Find a quiet place to read the Bible and pray. Memorize 2 Corinthians 4:8-9. Take time to smell some roses. Laugh with your family. God will replenish your inner strength. You'll be ready to face next week!

For more information or to place an order,
please contact your local Christian Bookstore
or:

103B Cannifton Road
Belleville, ON K8N 4V2

Phone (613) 962-2360; Fax (613) 962-3055
1-800-238-6376
Email: essence@intranet.on.ca
Internet: http://www.essence.on.ca

The following books are available from Essence Publishing:

A Sinner Meets the Saviour by Wayne MacLeod . . *85 pp, $8.95*
A study of encounters between Jesus and sinners in the Gospel of John and how these meetings caused people to re-examine and change their lives. This book will teach and challenge readers in their relationship with the Lord.

Olive Shoots Around Your Table by John Visser . *426 pp, $17.95*
Subtitled, *Raising Functional Kids in a Dysfunctional World*, this is a comprehensive manual on breaking the cycle of family dysfunction and raising healthy kids. Filled with practical insights, real life stories and helpful diagrams, this book is a must read for everyone who wants to understand the dynamics of family life.

Refiner's Fire by Reg Faust. . . . . *170 pp, $13.95*
This is the story of a man broken by the pain of rejection, abuse and his own failure and sin. Crushed beneath the apparent abandonment of God, he cries out in anguish as he loses both his family and his faith. Travel through the Psalms with this man as he searches and struggles through the fires of testing to find true healing.

From Tabernacle to Church by Dr. John Marcus. *156 pp, $13.95*
A deeper study of the Tabernacle and how it parallels the Church today in its service as the House of God. Contains many pictures and diagrams and study questions.

Handling Stress by John Visser . . . . *112 pp, $9.95*
To live is to experience stress. Some people cope very well with stress while others do not. This book discusses causes and symptoms of stress in today's world and gives practical advice on how to handle it.

A Lift for Living by Herman Kroeker . . . . *363 pp, $16.95*
A daily devotional for the whole year by a veteran servant of God. Filled with inspiring quotes, Scripture, prayers, stories & poems. Excellent for gift-giving & personal use.

And the Pink Snow Fell by Rev. Ray Cross . . . ***100 pp, $14.95***
This is the story of the Port Hope, ON, gas explosion of November 1993 and the huge impact it had on one of the families living adjacent to the site of the explosion. Contains many photographs. Excellent for grief therapy!

Protestant Church Growth in Korea by Dr. John Kim . ***364 pp, $39.95***
The Korean Church is one of the fastest growing churches in the world today. In this book, the author offers some insights into why this is so and examines some of the factors that have influenced this growth.

Controversy & Confusion by Herbert E. Holder . . . . . . ***275 pp, $23.75***
There are many different beliefs surrounding important doctrinal issues. This book addresses these conflicting beliefs and examines them under the microscope of Scripture to clarify what God really intended in His Word.

Binder of Wounds by Sini Den Otter . . . . ***129 pp, $11.95***
A medley of meditations describing some of the author's experiences as a hospital chaplain. Inspirational and honest, this book hopes to encourage believers in their daily struggles and give practical insights into caring for others.

Righteous Anger by Dr. Christopher Schrader . . ***180 pp, 16.95***
The negative effects of anger are reverberating across the entire global community. Examination of three examples in the Gospels and the opinions of various scholars give Christians concrete principles to follow for properly expressing anger — as Jesus did.

Whispers from Heaven by Gail Parks . . . . ***84 pp, $8.95***
A book of inspirational poetry that has touched the hearts of many people. It is the author's prayer that these words will encourage many, especially those who are suffering.

Desecrated Lands by Peter Pikkert. . . . . ***164 pp, $12.95***
This novel is a powerful portrayal of the inconsistencies that surround the various people-groups in the Middle East with regards to the gospel. Israel is God's chosen nation – does that mean Arabs and Muslims are His enemies?

Order Form

Ordered By: (please print)

Name: _____

Address: _____

City: _____ Prov./State: _____

Postal/Zip Code: _____ Telephone: _____

Please send me the following book(s): (All Prices in Cdn. Dollars.)

Qty.	Title	Unit Price	Total
_____	*The Wealthy Preacher*	$11.95	$_____
_____	*A Sinner meets the Saviour*	$8.95	$_____
_____	*Olive Shoots Around Your Table*	$17.95	$_____
_____	*Refiner's Fire*	$13.95	$_____
_____	*From Tabernacle to Church*	$13.95	$_____
_____	*Handling Stress*	$9.95	$_____
_____	*A Lift for Living*	$16.95	$_____
_____	*And the Pink Snow Fell*	$14.95	$_____
_____	*Protestant Church Growth in Korea*	$39.95	$_____
_____	*Binder of Wounds*	$11.95	$_____
_____	*Righteous Anger*	$16.95	$_____
_____	*Desecrated Lands*	$12.95	$_____

Shipping ($3.00 first book - $1.00 each add. book): $_____

G.S.T. @ 7%: $_____

Total: $_____

Payable by Cheque, Money Order or **VISA**

VISA #:_____ Expiry:_____

Signature:_____

✂ -

**To order by phone, call our toll-free number, 1-800-238-6376
and have your credit card handy.**